Math Achievement

Enriching Activities Based on NCTM Standards

Grade 1

by

Alison Shelton

Table of Contents

Introduction

Welcome to the **Math Achievement** series! Each book in this series is designed to reinforce the math skills appropriate for each grade level and to encourage high-level thinking and problem-solving skills. Enhancing students' thinking and problem-solving abilities can help them succeed in all academic areas. In addition, experiencing success in math can increase a student's confidence and self-esteem, both in and out of the classroom.

The following math skills are covered in this book:

- **problem solving**
- **place value**
- **addition**
- **subtraction**
- **regrouping**
- **fractional parts**
- **time**
- **calendar**
- **money**
- **measurement**
- **geometry**
- **charts and graphs**

Each **Math Achievement** book offers challenging questions **based on the standards specified by the National Council of Teachers of Mathematics (NCTM)**. All five content standards (number and operations, algebra, geometry, measurement, data analysis and probability) and the process standard, problem solving, are covered in the activities.

The questions and format are similar to those found on standardized math tests. The experience students gain from answering questions in this format may help increase their test scores.

These exercises can be used to enhance the regular math curriculum, to individualize instruction, to provide extra practice for home schoolers, or to review skills between grades.

Each **Math Achievement** book contains **four pretests in standardized test format** at the beginning of each book. The pretests have been designed so that they may be used individually, as four stand-alone tests, or in groups. They may be used to identify students' needs in specific areas, or to compare students' math abilities at the beginning and end of the school year. **A scoring box is also included on each activity page.** This scoring box can be programmed to suit your specific classroom and student needs with total problems, total correct, and score.

Name ________________________

Read the following problems. Circle the letter beside the correct answer in each question.

1. $3 + 5 =$ ____
   A. 6
   B. 9
   C. 8

2. $2 + 4 =$ ____
   A. 6
   B. 3
   C. 5

3. $7 + 0 =$ ____
   A. 2
   B. 7
   C. 8

4. $6 + 4 =$ ____
   A. 9
   B. 8
   C. 10

---

5. John's baseball team scored 3 runs in the first inning, 2 in the third inning, and 1 in the seventh inning. How many runs did they score in all?

   A. 5 B. 6 C. 9 D. 10

6. Greg's mom bought 12 oatmeal cookies and 12 chocolate chip cookies. How many cookies did she buy in all?

   A. 24 B. 18 C. 22 D. 19

---

7. $3 + 5 + 1 =$ ____
   A. 10
   B. 9
   C. 11

8. $2 + 0 + 8 =$ ____
   A. 9
   B. 11
   C. 10

---

9. $\begin{array}{r} 24 \\ +33 \\ \hline \end{array}$
   A. 57
   B. 68
   C. 75

10. $\begin{array}{r} 49 \\ +20 \\ \hline \end{array}$
   A. 70
   B. 69
   C. 59

Total Problems:	Total Correct:	Score:

Name ______________________

Read the following problems. Circle the letter beside the correct answer in each question.

1. $368 + 331$ — A. 669 B. 399 C. 699

2. $742 + 106$ — A. 862 B. 848 C. 768

---

3. 8 − 3 = ____ — A. 8 B. 7 C. 5

4. 18 − 9 = ____ — A. 8 B. 9 C. 10

5. 12 − 6 = ____ — A. 5 B. 6 C. 10

6. 8 − 0 = ____ — A. 0 B. 1 C. 8

---

7. Julie had 20 beads on a string, but she lost 7 of them. How many beads were left?

   A. 17 B. 13 C. 7 D. 11

8. Joe had 35 baseball cards. He gave 10 to Tony. How many cards did Joe have left?

   A. 9 B. 25 C. 10 D. 15

---

9. $49 - 26$ — A. 13 B. 26 C. 23

10. $592 - 121$ — A. 521 B. 463 C. 471

Total Problems:	Total Correct:	Score:

Name ______________________________ **Pretest**

Read the following problems. Circle the letter beside the correct answer in each question.

1. How many parts does the bar have?

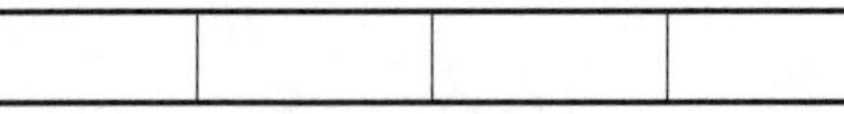

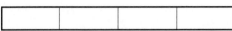

A. 4 B. 8 C. 7 D. 1

2. How much of the bar is shaded?

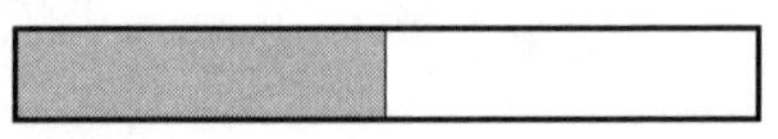

A. $\frac{1}{2}$ B. all C. $\frac{1}{4}$ D. none

---

3. How many sets of ten and how many ones are in this group of circles?

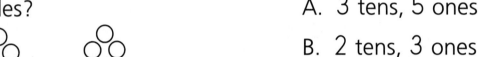

A. 3 tens, 5 ones

B. 2 tens, 3 ones

C. 3 tens, 7 ones

---

4. What time does the clock show?

A. 9:00

B. 9:30

C. 2:00

5. What time does the clock show?

A. 8:00

B. 2:00

C. 5:30

6. Which clock shows 6:00?

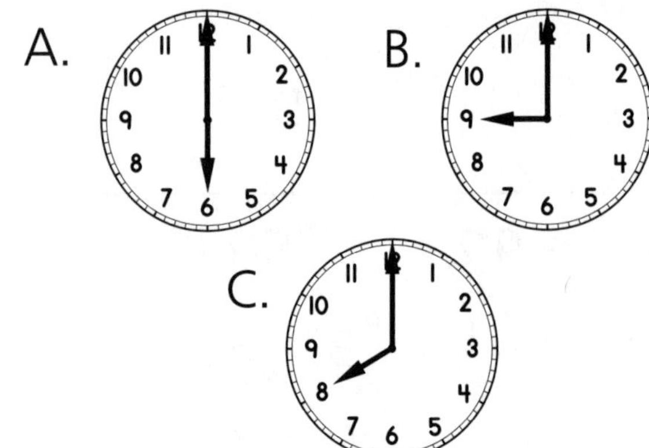

7. Molly started her homework at 4:00. It took her 30 minutes to finish. Which clock shows when she finished?

Total Problems: Total Correct: Score:

Name ______________________________

Read the following problems. Circle the letter beside the correct answer in each question.

1. How much money is shown?

A. 19¢ B. 24¢ C. 27¢

2. How much money is shown?

A. 15¢ B. 16¢ C. 25¢

April

Sunday	Monday	Tuesday	Wednesday	Thursday	Friday	Saturday
	1	2	3	4	5	6
7	8	9	10	11	12	13
14	15	16	17	18	19	20
21	22	23	24	25	26	27
28	29	30				

3. On what day does the month start?

A. Monday B. Wednesday C. Friday

4. How many Tuesdays are in this month?

A. 1 B. 2 C. 5

5. Which date is not a Wednesday?

A. 10 B. 24 C. 27

Total Problems: **Total Correct:** **Score:**

Pretest Answer Key

Name ____________________ **Pretest**

Read the following problems. Circle the letter beside the correct answer in each question.

1. 3 + 5 = ____ A. 6 B. 9 **C. 8**
2. 2 + 4 = ____ **A. 6** B. 3 C. 5
3. 7 + 0 = ____ A. 2 **B. 7** C. 8
4. 6 + 4 = ____ A. 9 B. 8 **C. 10**
5. John's baseball team scored 3 runs in the first inning, 2 in the third inning, and 1 in the seventh inning. How many runs did they score in all?
   A. 5 **B. 6** C. 9 D. 10
6. Greg's mom bought 12 oatmeal cookies and 12 chocolate chip cookies. How many cookies did she buy in all?
   A. 24 B. 18 C. 22 D. 19
7. 3 + 5 + 1 = ____ A. 10 **B. 9** C. 11
8. 2 + 0 + 8 = ____ A. 9 B. 11 **C. 10**
9. 24 + 33 **A. 57** B. 68 C. 75
10. 49 + 20 A. 70 **B. 69** C. 59

4 | Total Problems: | Total Correct: | Score:

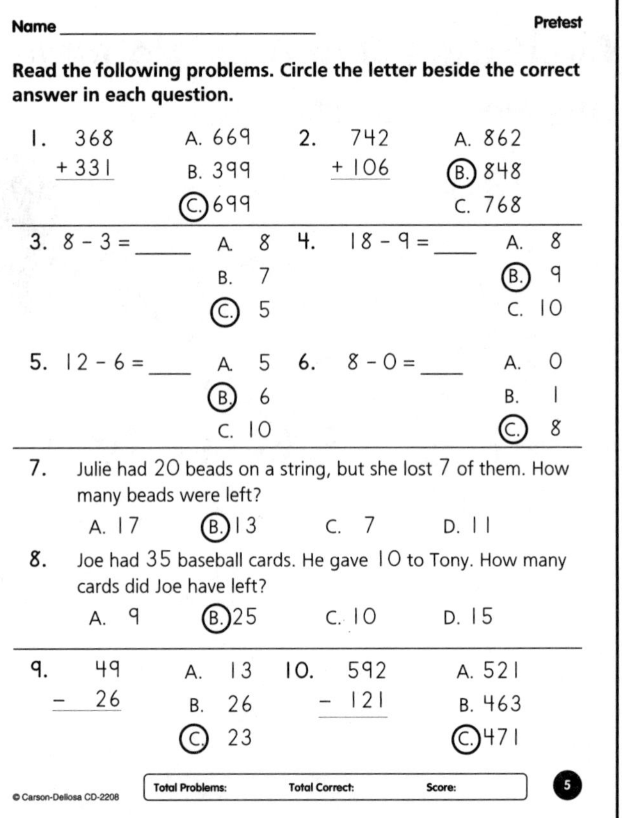

Name ____________________ **Pretest**

Read the following problems. Circle the letter beside the correct answer in each question.

1. 368 + 331 A. 669 B. 399 **C. 699**
2. 742 + 106 A. 862 **B. 848** C. 768
3. 8 − 3 = ____ A. 8 B. 7 **C. 5**
4. 18 − 9 = ____ A. 8 **B. 9** C. 10
5. 12 − 6 = ____ A. 5 **B. 6** C. 10
6. 8 − 0 = ____ A. 0 B. 1 **C. 8**
7. Julie had 20 beads on a string, but she lost 7 of them. How many beads were left?
   A. 17 **B. 13** C. 7 D. 11
8. Joe had 35 baseball cards. He gave 10 to Tony. How many cards did Joe have left?
   A. 9 **B. 25** C. 10 D. 15
9. 49 − 26 A. 13 B. 26 **C. 23**
10. 592 − 121 A. 521 B. 463 **C. 471**

© Carson-Dellosa CD-2208 | Total Problems: | Total Correct: | Score: | 5

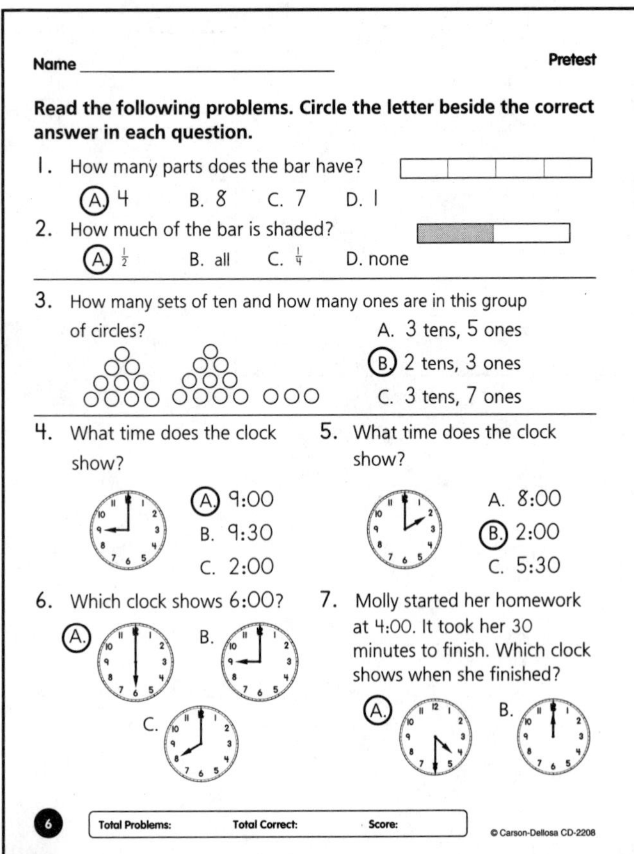

Name ____________________ **Pretest**

Read the following problems. Circle the letter beside the correct answer in each question.

1. How many parts does the bar have?
   A. 4 B. 8 C. 7 D. 1
2. How much of the bar is shaded?
   A. $\frac{1}{2}$ B. all C. $\frac{1}{4}$ D. none
3. How many sets of ten and how many ones are in this group of circles?
   A. 3 tens, 5 ones **B. 2 tens, 3 ones** C. 3 tens, 7 ones
4. What time does the clock show?
   A. 9:00 B. 9:30 C. 2:00
5. What time does the clock show?
   A. 8:00 **B. 2:00** C. 5:30
6. Which clock shows 6:00?
   A. B. C.
7. Molly started her homework at 4:00. It took her 30 minutes to finish. Which clock shows when she finished?
   A. B.

6 | Total Problems: | Total Correct: | Score: | © Carson-Dellosa CD-2208

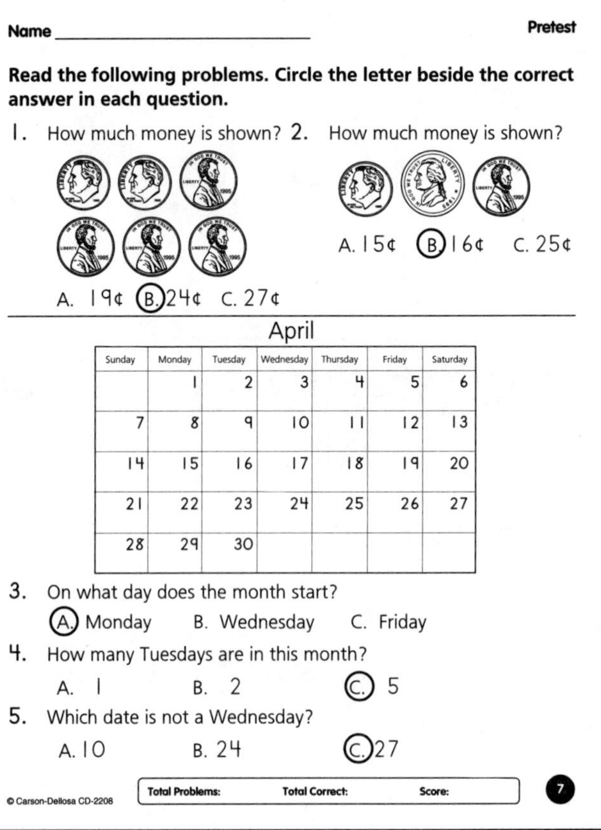

Name ____________________ **Pretest**

Read the following problems. Circle the letter beside the correct answer in each question.

1. How much money is shown?
   A. 19¢ **B. 24¢** C. 27¢
2. How much money is shown?
   A. 15¢ **B. 16¢** C. 25¢

April

Sunday	Monday	Tuesday	Wednesday	Thursday	Friday	Saturday
	1	2	3	4	5	6
7	8	9	10	11	12	13
14	15	16	17	18	19	20
21	22	23	24	25	26	27
28	29	30				

3. On what day does the month start?
   A. Monday B. Wednesday C. Friday
4. How many Tuesdays are in this month?
   A. 1 B. 2 **C. 5**
5. Which date is not a Wednesday?
   A. 10 B. 24 **C. 27**

© Carson-Dellosa CD-2208 | Total Problems: | Total Correct: | Score: | 7

Name ______________________________

Circle sets of ten. Write how many tens and ones in each place-value table. Write the number on the line underneath.

1.

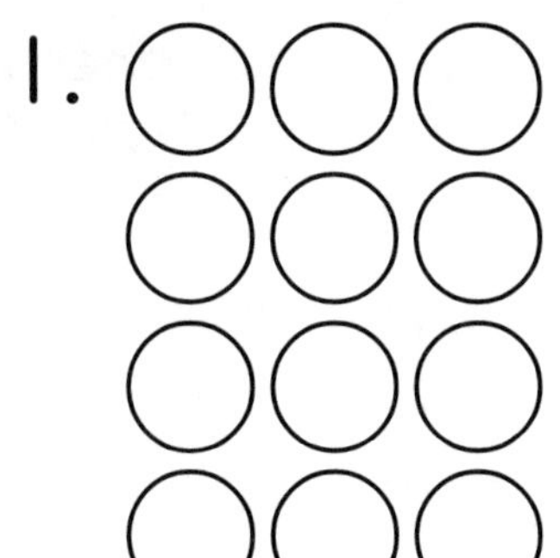

tens	ones

____

2.

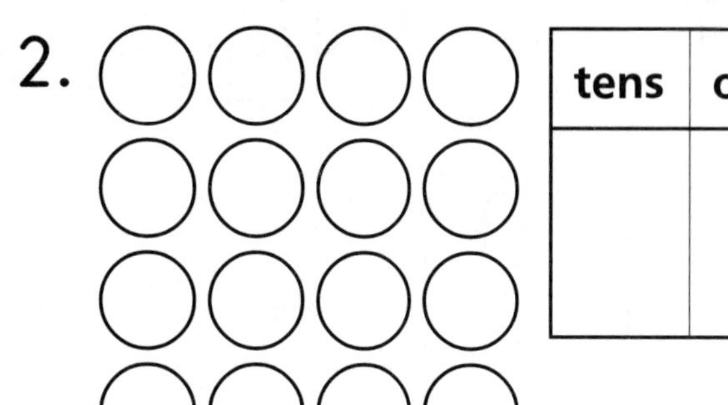

tens	ones

____

3.

tens	ones

____

4.

tens	ones

____

5. Write a number between 10 and 20 on the line below. Draw balls in the empty space below to show the number. Then, write how many tens and ones in the place-value table.

Number: _____

tens	ones

Total Problems: Total Correct: Score:

Name ______________________

Write how many tens and ones in each place-value table. Write the number on the line underneath.

1. 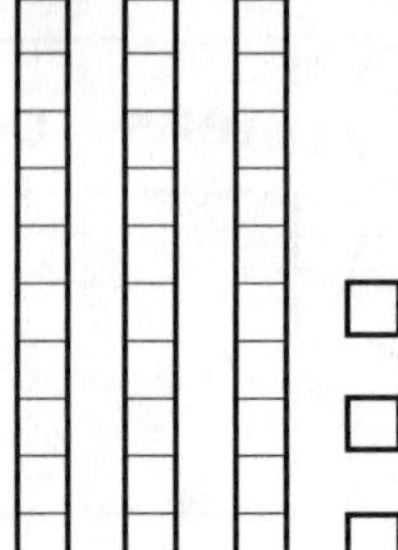

tens	ones

____

2. 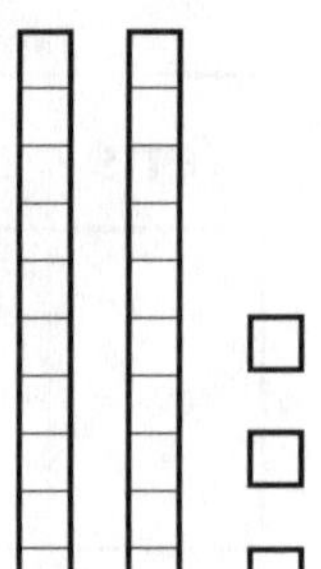

tens	ones

____

3.

tens	ones

____

4.

tens	ones

____

5.

tens	ones

____

6.

tens	ones

____

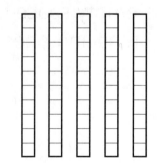

Total Problems: Total Correct: Score:

Name ____________________

Study the box below. Solve each problem and write the answer in the space below it.

Rule: Addition is combining the values of 2 numbers to find the sum.	**Example:** 3 + 1 = 4	**Think to Yourself:** Draw out the numbers and then count them all.

1. 3 + 1
2. 5 + 1
3. 1 + 1
4. 4 + 1
5. 2 + 1
6. 0 + 6
7. 4 + 2
8. 2 + 3
9. 3 + 2
10. 2 + 4
11. 2 + 2
12. 3 + 3
13. 4 + 0
14. 1 + 5
15. 6 + 0
16. 0 + 5
17. 1 + 2
18. 1 + 3
19. 5 + 0
20. 1 + 4

Total Problems: Total Correct: Score:

Name ____________________

Solve each problem and write the answer on the line beside it.

1. 5 + 1 = ____ 2. 3 + 3 = ____ 3. 6 + 0 = ____

4. 2 + 2 = ____ 5. 0 + 0 = ____ 6. 1 + 2 = ____

7. 1 + 3 = ____ 8. 4 + 1 = ____ 9. 5 + 0 = ____

10. 2 + 4 = ____ 11. 3 + 1 = ____ 12. 4 + 2 = ____

13. 3 + 0 = ____ 14. 0 + 6 = ____ 15. 3 + 2 = ____

16. 4 + 1 = ____ 17. 1 + 1 = ____ 18. 2 + 1 = ____

19. 0 + 4 = ____ 20. 1 + 5 = ____ 21. 2 + 3 = ____

Total Problems: Total Correct: Score:

Name ______________________________

Solve each problem and write the answer in the space below it.

1. $5 + 3$
2. $7 + 1$
3. $8 + 0$
4. $5 + 1$
5. $2 + 5$
6. $2 + 6$
7. $5 + 5$
8. $6 + 2$
9. $3 + 6$
10. $4 + 4$
11. $3 + 3$
12. $1 + 1$
13. $4 + 3$
14. $5 + 4$
15. $2 + 2$
16. $5 + 0$
17. $3 + 5$
18. $3 + 7$
19. $2 + 3$
20. $6 + 4$
21. $7 + 2$
22. $9 + 1$
23. $1 + 7$
24. $0 + 6$
25. $8 + 2$

Total Problems:	Total Correct:	Score:

Name ______________________________

Solve each problem and write the answer on the line beside it.

1. 2 + 6 = ____	2. 3 + 5 = ____	3. 5 + 5 = ____
4. 6 + 3 = ____	5. 0 + 1 = ____	6. 2 + 1 = ____
7. 10 + 0 = ____	8. 3 + 6 = ____	9. 4 + 5 = ____
10. 4 + 6 = ____	11. 9 + 0 = ____	12. 5 + 2 = ____
13. 4 + 1 = ____	14. 7 + 2 = ____	15. 8 + 2 = ____
16. 1 + 6 = ____	17. 1 + 3 = ____	18. 0 + 8 = ____
19. 6 + 2 = ____	20. 0 + 9 = ____	21. 4 + 3 = ____
22. 3 + 7 = ____	23. 0 + 4 = ____	24. 8 + 1 = ____
25. 4 + 4 = ____	26. 7 + 1 = ____	27. 7 + 0 = ____

Total Problems: **Total Correct:** **Score:**

Name ______________________________

Study the box below. Find each sum and write the answer on the line beside it. Then, change the order and write a new number sentence.

Rule: When you add, the order of the numbers does not change the answer.	**Example:** $2 + 1 = \underline{3}$ $1 + 2 = \underline{3}$

1. $1 + 3 =$ ____ ____ + ____ = ____

2. $4 + 6 =$ ____ ____ + ____ = ____

3. $7 + 3 =$ ____ ____ + ____ = ____

4. $2 + 3 =$ ____ ____ + ____ = ____

5. $9 + 1 =$ ____ ____ + ____ = ____

6. $8 + 0 =$ ____ ____ + ____ = ____

7. $2 + 3 =$ ____ ____ + ____ = ____

Total Problems: **Total Correct:** **Score:**

Name ______________________________

Study the example below. Use the number line to add. Circle the greater number. Draw ⌒ to count on. Write the answer on the line beside it.

Example:

3 + 5 = 8

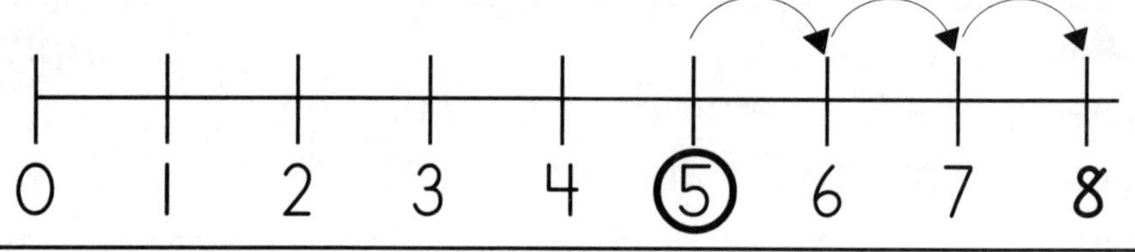

1. 2 + 4 = ____

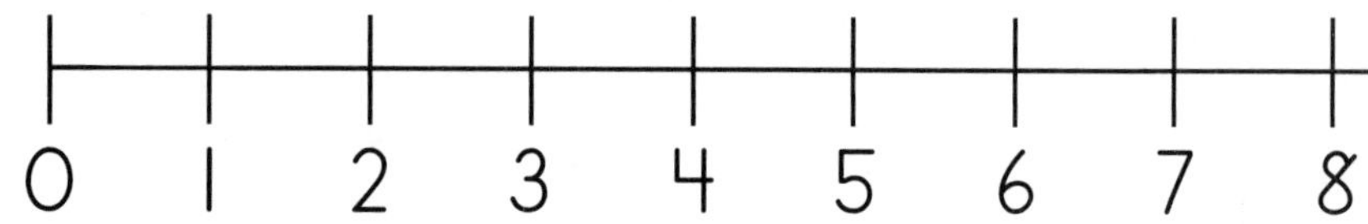

2. 6 + 2 = ____

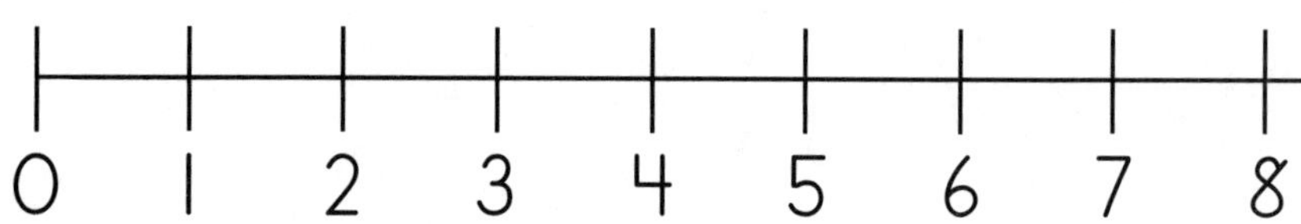

3. 5 + 1 = ____

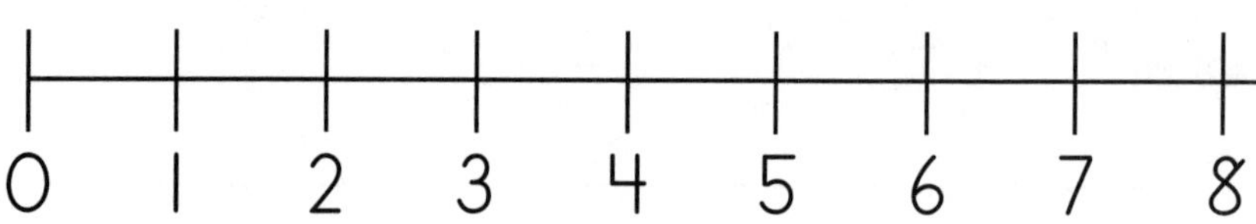

4. 3 + 3 = ____

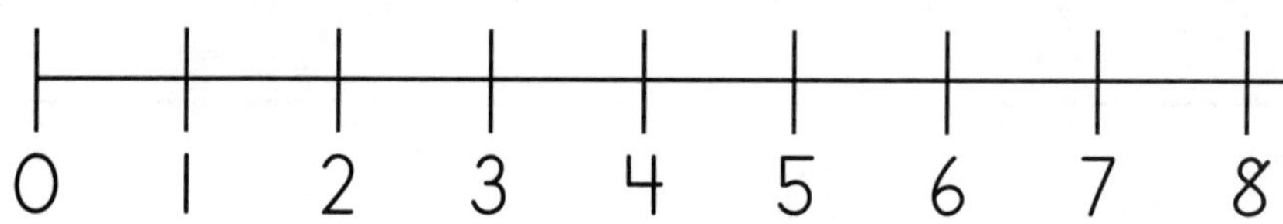

5. 1 + 4 = ____

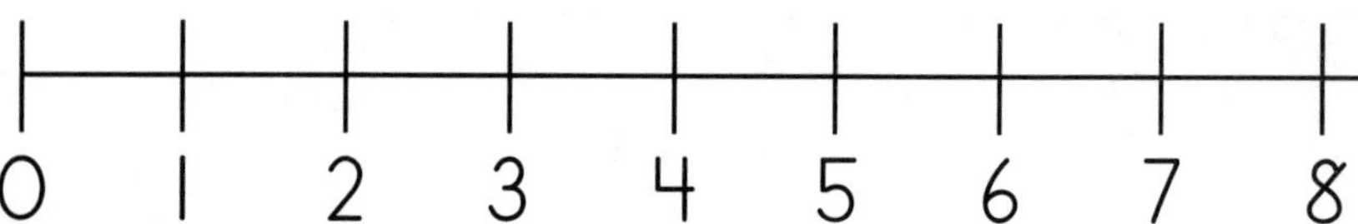

Total Problems: **Total Correct:** **Score:**

Name ____________________

Study the example below. Solve each problem. Write the answer on the line beside it.

Example:	**Think to Yourself:**
2 + 6 = 8	Circle the greater number and count on. Start with 6 and count up 2.

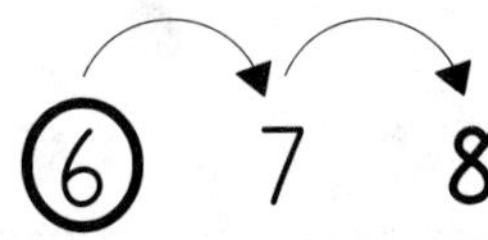

1. 5 + 2 = ____
2. 8 + 2 = ____
3. 10 + 0 = ____
4. 7 + 2 = ____
5. 4 + 6 = ____
6. 4 + 4 = ____
7. 2 + 5 = ____
8. 6 + 3 = ____
9. 9 + 1 = ____
10. 7 + 3 = ____
11. 3 + 5 = ____
12. 3 + 4 = ____
13. 5 + 1 = ____
14. 5 + 2 = ____
15. 4 + 5 = ____

Total Problems:	Total Correct:	Score:

Name ______________________

Study the example below. Draw one or more ● to make doubles. Write each number sentence on the lines below it.

Example:

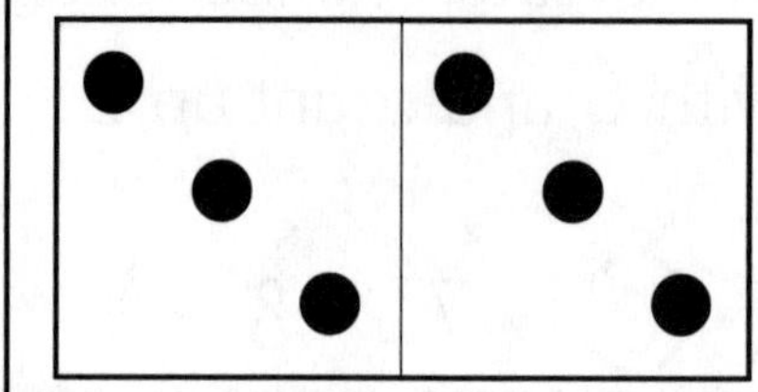

3 + 3 = 6

1. 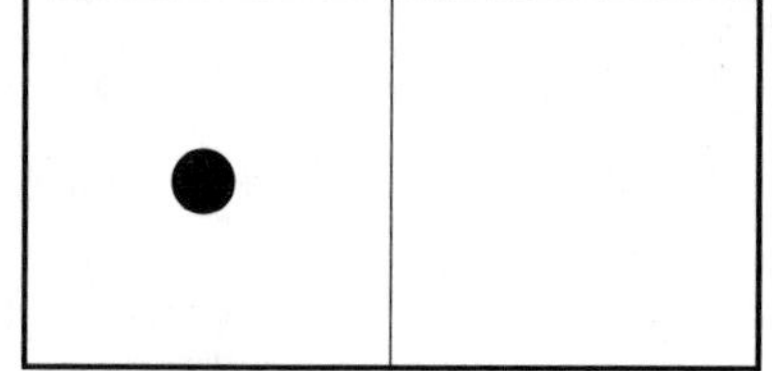

____ + ____ = ____

2. 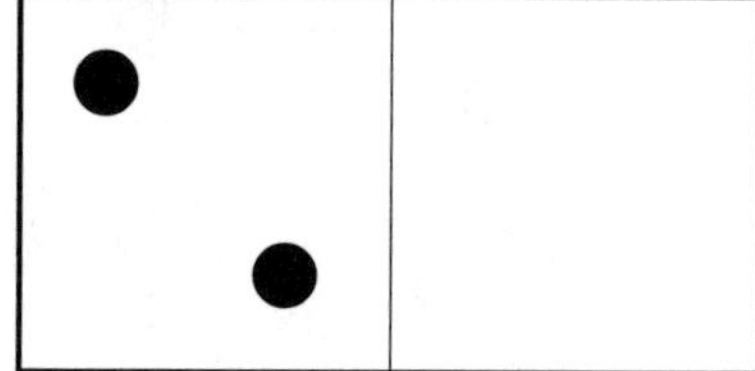

____ + ____ = ____

3. 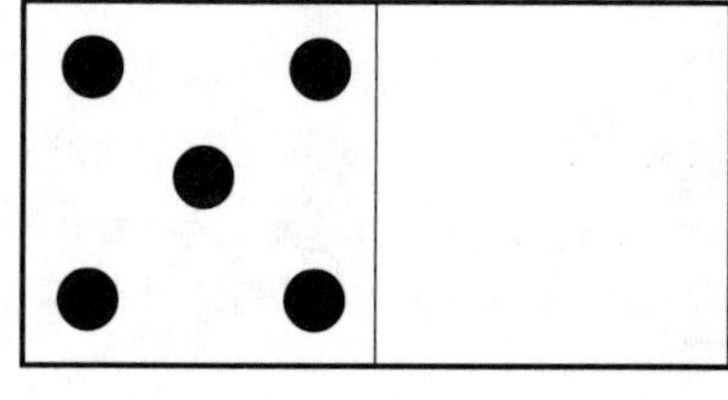

____ + ____ = ____

4. 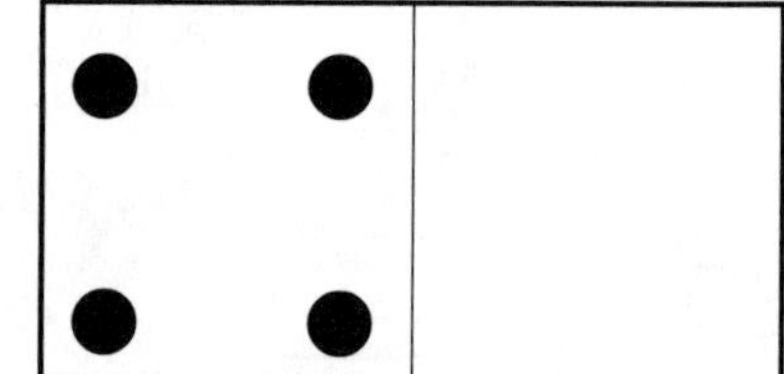

____ + ____ = ____

Draw your own ● in the boxes. Write each number sentence on the lines below it.

5. 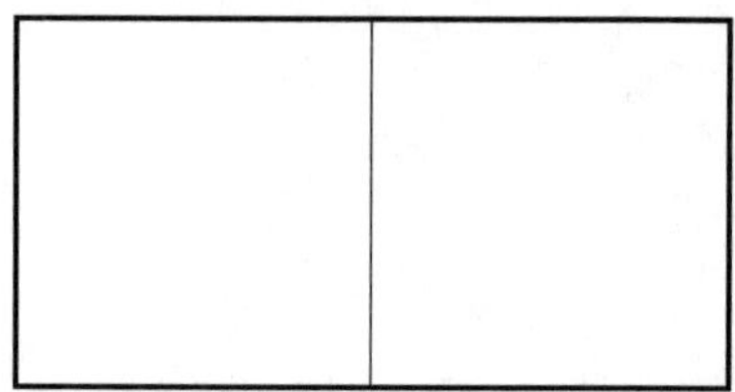

____ + ____ = ____

6. 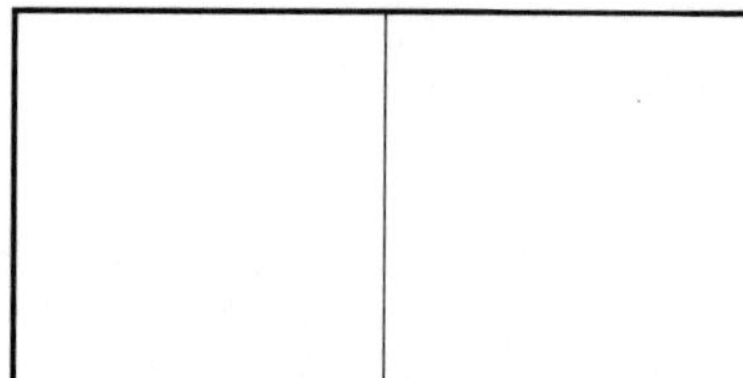

____ + ____ = ____

Total Problems: **Total Correct:** **Score:**

Name ______________________________

Solve each problem and write the answer in the space below it.

1.	2.	3.	4.	5.
7 + 8	9 + 5	8 + 5	5 + 7	2 + 9

6.	7.	8.	9.	10.
7 + 3	6 + 9	9 + 1	8 + 6	4 + 9

11.	12.	13.	14.	15.
4 + 8	7 + 7	3 + 8	6 + 5	6 + 4

16.	17.	18.	19.	20.
5 + 4	1 + 9	6 + 6	4 + 4	3 + 7

21.	22.	23.	24.	25.
7 + 6	5 + 9	6 + 3	9 + 6	5 + 6

Total Problems: **Total Correct:** **Score:**

Name ______________________________

Solve each problem and write the answer in the space below it.

1. $7 + 9$	2. $6 + 6$	3. $5 + 8$	4. $9 + 7$	5. $9 + 9$
6. $8 + 6$	7. $8 + 7$	8. $8 + 9$	9. $10 + 9$	10. $7 + 8$
11. $5 + 5$	12. $8 + 5$	13. $10 + 4$	14. $9 + 5$	15. $8 + 4$
16. $9 + 1$	17. $3 + 9$	18. $6 + 9$	19. $7 + 6$	20. $5 + 9$
21. $9 + 8$	22. $7 + 7$	23. $7 + 5$	24. $6 + 7$	25. $3 + 8$

Total Problems: Total Correct: Score:

Name ____________________

Solve each problem and write the answer on the line beside it.

1. 7 + 6 = ____ 2. 8 + 1 = ____ 3. 3 + 5 = ____

4. 9 + 9 = ____ 5. 6 + 3 = ____ 6. 7 + 4 = ____

7. 10 + 9 = ____ 8. 10 + 10 = ____ 9. 5 + 5 = ____

10. 8 + 6 = ____ 11. 6 + 9 = ____ 12. 9 + 8 = ____

13. 2 + 7 = ____ 14. 8 + 8 = ____ 15. 7 + 8 = ____

16. 8 + 4 = ____ 17. 9 + 6 = ____ 18. 7 + 3 = ____

19. 8 + 7 = ____ 20. 6 + 8 = ____ 21. 4 + 9 = ____

22. 6 + 5 = ____ 23. 9 + 7 = ____ 24. 2 + 8 = ____

25. 4 + 9 = ____ 26. 8 + 5 = ____ 27. 10 + 8 = ____

Total Problems: Total Correct: Score:

Name ______________________________

Solve each problem and write the answer in the space below it.

1.	2.	3.	4.	5.
8	6	8	6	4
9	5	8	6	8
+ 1	+ 2	+ 2	+ 4	+ 1

6.	7.	8.	9.	10.
3	7	2	7	1
6	8	2	4	6
+ 2	+ 3	+ 8	+ 2	+ 5

11.	12.	13.	14.	15.
4	9	8	5	3
4	8	4	5	3
+ 5	+ 1	+ 4	+ 5	+ 5

16.	17.	18.	19.	20.
4	1	6	7	5
7	2	1	2	3
+ 2	+ 4	+ 9	+ 6	+ 9

Total Problems: **Total Correct:** **Score:**

Name ______________________________

Solve each problem and write the answer in the space below it.

1.	2.	3.	4.	5.
8	5	7	5	3
7	4	7	5	7
+ 2	+ 1	+ 1	+ 3	+ 0

6.	7.	8.	9.	10.
2	6	1	6	0
5	7	1	3	5
+ 1	+ 2	+ 7	+ 1	+ 1

11.	12.	13.	14.	15.
3	8	7	4	3
3	7	3	4	2
+ 4	+ 2	+ 4	+ 4	+ 4

16.	17.	18.	19.	20.
3	5	5	6	4
6	3	2	1	2
+ 4	+ 6	+ 8	+ 5	+ 8

Total Problems: **Total Correct:** **Score:**

Name ______________________________

Solve each problem and write the answer in the space below it.

1.	2.	3.	4.	5.
9	7	9	7	5
8	6	9	7	9
+ 3	+ 3	+ 3	+ 5	+ 2

6.	7.	8.	9.	10.
4	8	3	8	2
7	2	3	3	7
+ 3	+ 4	+ 9	+ 1	+ 6

11.	12.	13.	14.	15.
6	8	9	6	4
5	9	5	7	4
+ 6	+ 4	+ 5	+ 7	+ 6

16.	17.	18.	19.	20.
5	2	7	8	6
8	3	2	3	4
+ 3	+ 5	+ 8	+ 7	+ 7

Total Problems: Total Correct: Score:

Name ______________________________

Study the example below. Then, solve each problem and write the missing number in the box.

Example:	**Think to Yourself:**
$7 + \boxed{7} = 14$	7 plus what number equals 14?

1. $9 + \square = 17$
2. $3 + \square = 10$
3. $8 + \square = 14$
4. $6 + \square = 12$
5. $5 + \square = 10$
6. $4 + \square = 13$
7. $3 + \square = 11$
8. $6 + \square = 13$
9. $9 + \square = 14$
10. $8 + \square = 16$
11. $7 + \square = 12$
12. $8 + \square = 13$
13. $3 + \square = 12$
14. $5 + \square = 14$
15. $7 + \square = 11$
16. $5 + \square = 9$
17. $6 + \square = 13$
18. $9 + \square = 18$
19. $4 + \square = 11$
20. $8 + \square = 17$

Total Problems: **Total Correct:** **Score:**

Name ______________________________

Two-Digit Addition without Regrouping

Study the box below. Solve each problem and write the answer in the space below it.

Rule:	**Example:**
Draw a line between the tens and the ones places. Add the ones first, then add the tens.	$\begin{array}{r} 1\vert 5 \\ +\ 2\vert 0 \\ \hline 3\vert 5 \end{array}$

1. $\begin{array}{r} 30 \\ +25 \\ \hline \end{array}$ 2. $\begin{array}{r} 16 \\ +13 \\ \hline \end{array}$ 3. $\begin{array}{r} 24 \\ +14 \\ \hline \end{array}$ 4. $\begin{array}{r} 12 \\ +14 \\ \hline \end{array}$ 5. $\begin{array}{r} 19 \\ +10 \\ \hline \end{array}$

6. $\begin{array}{r} 54 \\ +\ 2 \\ \hline \end{array}$ 7. $\begin{array}{r} 60 \\ +30 \\ \hline \end{array}$ 8. $\begin{array}{r} 15 \\ +14 \\ \hline \end{array}$ 9. $\begin{array}{r} 22 \\ +33 \\ \hline \end{array}$ 10. $\begin{array}{r} 40 \\ +30 \\ \hline \end{array}$

11. $\begin{array}{r} 36 \\ +22 \\ \hline \end{array}$ 12. $\begin{array}{r} 15 \\ +21 \\ \hline \end{array}$ 13. $\begin{array}{r} 60 \\ +20 \\ \hline \end{array}$ 14. $\begin{array}{r} 18 \\ +10 \\ \hline \end{array}$ 15. $\begin{array}{r} 40 \\ +17 \\ \hline \end{array}$

16. $\begin{array}{r} 21 \\ +70 \\ \hline \end{array}$ 17. $\begin{array}{r} 30 \\ +25 \\ \hline \end{array}$ 18. $\begin{array}{r} 56 \\ +41 \\ \hline \end{array}$ 19. $\begin{array}{r} 32 \\ +32 \\ \hline \end{array}$ 20. $\begin{array}{r} 50 \\ +25 \\ \hline \end{array}$

Total Problems: **Total Correct:** **Score:**

Name ______________________

Two-Digit Addition without Regrouping

Solve each problem and write the answer in the space below it.

1. 23 + 53 =
2. 41 + 43 =
3. 88 + 10 =
4. 77 + 12 =
5. 17 + 22 =
6. 14 + 64 =
7. 12 + 12 =
8. 82 + 13 =
9. 47 + 31 =
10. 68 + 10 =
11. 55 + 10 =
12. 82 + 14 =
13. 62 + 24 =
14. 80 + 10 =
15. 40 + 23 =
16. 50 + 31 =
17. 73 + 11 =
18. 25 + 12 =
19. 15 + 14 =
20. 25 + 33 =
21. 72 + 20 =
22. 52 + 40 =
23. 67 + 21 =
24. 23 + 11 =
25. 40 + 15 =

Total Problems: **Total Correct:** **Score:**

Name ______________________________

Three-Digit Addition without Regrouping

Solve each problem and write the answer in the space below it.

1. 231 + 222	2. 190 + 200	3. 362 + 322	4. 130 + 160
5. 300 + 200	6. 445 + 223	7. 110 + 320	8. 600 + 300
9. 303 + 404	10. 222 + 222	11. 661 + 331	12. 710 + 250
13. 437 + 562	14. 350 + 200	15. 500 + 250	16. 162 + 201
17. 656 + 333	18. 536 + 232	19. 432 + 234	20. 123 + 456
21. 710 + 213	22. 242 + 314	23. 534 + 225	24. 472 + 222

Total Problems: Total Correct: Score:

Name ______________________________

Three-Digit Addition without Regrouping

Solve each problem and write the answer in the space below it.

1. 630 + 240	2. 400 + 200	3. 800 + 100	4. 505 + 252
5. 741 + 147	6. 460 + 222	7. 725 + 250	8. 450 + 333
9. 188 + 200	10. 124 + 421	11. 461 + 120	12. 720 + 160
13. 250 + 235	14. 426 + 123	15. 836 + 121	16. 625 + 124
17. 816 + 142	18. 670 + 200	19. 231 + 231	20. 446 + 222
21. 809 + 100	22. 752 + 231	23. 690 + 209	24. 489 + 510

Total Problems: **Total Correct:** **Score:**

Name ______________________________

Add to each picture to help solve the problem. Write the number sentence below.

1. Sally picks 2 flowers. Then, she picks 2 more. How many flowers does she have in all?

____ + ____ = ____

2. Scott picks 6 apples. Then, he picks 1 more. How many apples does he have in all?

____ + ____ = ____

3. Joe sees 2 fish bowls. There are 3 fish in each bowl. How many fish are there?

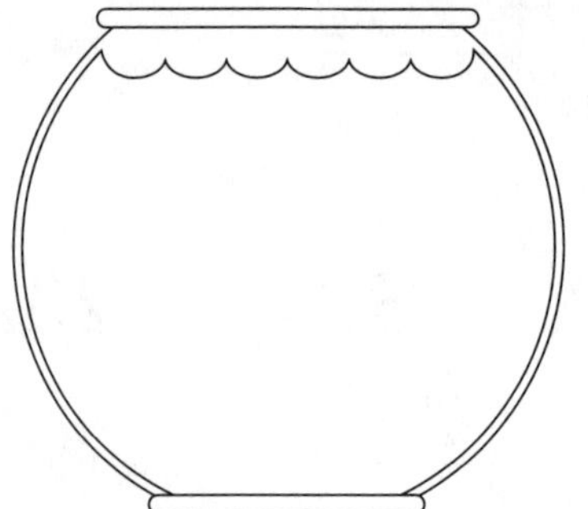

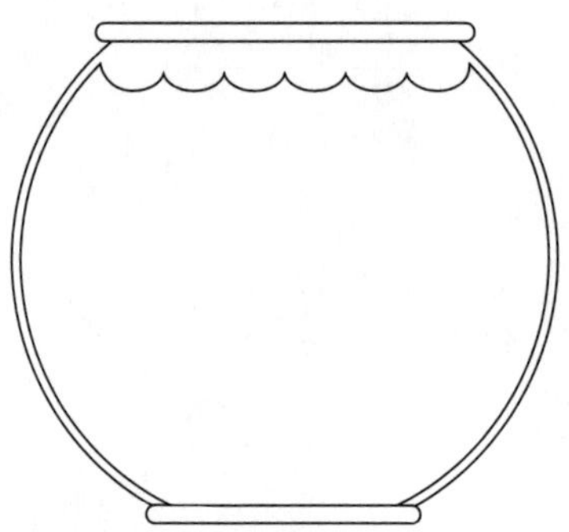

____ + ____ = ____

Total Problems:	Total Correct:	Score:

Name ____________________

Study the box below. Solve each problem and write the answer in the space below it.

Rule:	**Example:**	**Think to Yourself:**
Subtraction is taking away the value of one number from another number to find the difference.	$\begin{array}{r} 4 \\ -\ 1 \\ \hline 3 \end{array}$	Draw out the greater number and then take away the lesser number.

1. $\begin{array}{r} 6 \\ -\ 1 \\ \hline \end{array}$
2. $\begin{array}{r} 4 \\ -\ 2 \\ \hline \end{array}$
3. $\begin{array}{r} 3 \\ -\ 1 \\ \hline \end{array}$
4. $\begin{array}{r} 5 \\ -\ 0 \\ \hline \end{array}$
5. $\begin{array}{r} 5 \\ -\ 2 \\ \hline \end{array}$
6. $\begin{array}{r} 6 \\ -\ 6 \\ \hline \end{array}$
7. $\begin{array}{r} 4 \\ -\ 1 \\ \hline \end{array}$
8. $\begin{array}{r} 6 \\ -\ 4 \\ \hline \end{array}$
9. $\begin{array}{r} 4 \\ -\ 3 \\ \hline \end{array}$
10. $\begin{array}{r} 3 \\ -\ 2 \\ \hline \end{array}$
11. $\begin{array}{r} 6 \\ -\ 5 \\ \hline \end{array}$
12. $\begin{array}{r} 6 \\ -\ 3 \\ \hline \end{array}$
13. $\begin{array}{r} 1 \\ -\ 1 \\ \hline \end{array}$
14. $\begin{array}{r} 5 \\ -\ 3 \\ \hline \end{array}$
15. $\begin{array}{r} 4 \\ -\ 0 \\ \hline \end{array}$
16. $\begin{array}{r} 5 \\ -\ 4 \\ \hline \end{array}$
17. $\begin{array}{r} 6 \\ -\ 2 \\ \hline \end{array}$
18. $\begin{array}{r} 5 \\ -\ 1 \\ \hline \end{array}$
19. $\begin{array}{r} 5 \\ -\ 5 \\ \hline \end{array}$
20. $\begin{array}{r} 3 \\ -\ 3 \\ \hline \end{array}$

Total Problems: **Total Correct:** **Score:**

Name ____________________

Solve each problem and write the answer on the line beside it.

1. 2 – 2 = ____ 2. 6 – 1 = ____ 3. 4 – 2 = ____

4. 0 – 0 = ____ 5. 5 – 4 = ____ 6. 6 – 3 = ____

7. 5 – 2 = ____ 8. 3 – 2 = ____ 9. 6 – 4 = ____

10. 4 – 3 = ____ 11. 3 – 0 = ____ 12. 5 – 1 = ____

13. 1 – 0 = ____ 14. 2 – 1 = ____ 15. 3 – 1 = ____

16. 5 – 0 = ____ 17. 5 – 2 = ____ 18. 6 – 6 = ____

19. 4 – 1 = ____ 20. 6 – 0 = ____ 21. 5 – 3 = ____

22. 6 – 2 = ____ 23. 4 – 0 = ____ 24. 6 – 5 = ____

Total Problems: **Total Correct:** **Score:**

Name ______________________________

Solve each problem and write the answer in the space below it.

1.	2.	3.	4.	5.
10 − 2	8 − 5	9 − 6	7 − 6	7 − 7

6.	7.	8.	9.	10.
8 − 6	7 − 3	8 − 4	9 − 9	9 − 2

11.	12.	13.	14.	15.
7 − 5	6 − 5	8 − 3	9 − 4	10 − 8

16.	17.	18.	19.	20.
4 − 4	8 − 7	9 − 5	8 − 2	10 − 10

21.	22.	23.	24.	25.
5 − 4	6 − 2	10 − 3	9 − 3	10 − 5

Total Problems: Total Correct: Score:

Name ____________________

Solve each problem and write the answer on the line beside it.

1. 9 – 5 = ____ 2. 3 – 3 = ____ 3. 8 – 5 = ____

4. 7 – 5 = ____ 5. 8 – 6 = ____ 6. 8 – 4 = ____

7. 7 – 3 = ____ 8. 10 – 8 = ____ 9. 5 – 3 = ____

10. 7 – 4 = ____ 11. 6 – 5 = ____ 12. 8 – 4 = ____

13. 6 – 2 = ____ 14. 8 – 7 = ____ 15. 10 – 5 = ____

16. 4 – 2 = ____ 17. 8 – 3 = ____ 18. 10 – 6 = ____

19. 6 – 3 = ____ 20. 10 – 3 = ____ 21. 9 – 4 = ____

22. 9 – 1 = ____ 23. 10 – 2 = ____ 24. 0 – 0 = ____

25. 8 – 8 = ____ 26. 10 – 9 = ____ 27. 6 – 4 = ____

Total Problems: Total Correct: Score:

Name ______________________________

Study the box below. Use the number line to subtract. Circle the greater number. Draw ↶ to count back. Then, write the answer on the line provided.

Example:

8 – 5 = 3

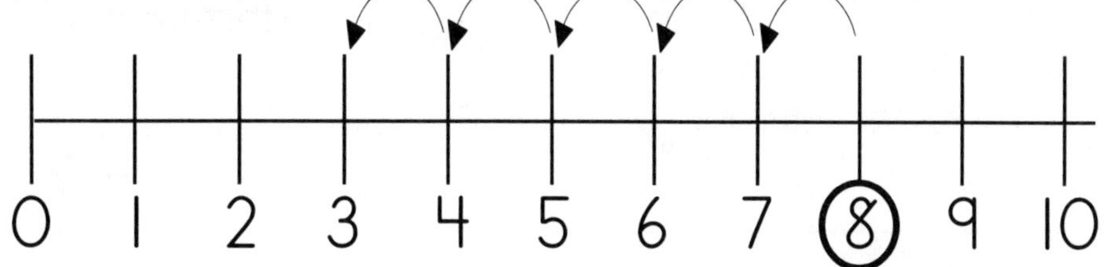

1. 10 – 6 = ____

2. 8 – 2 = ____

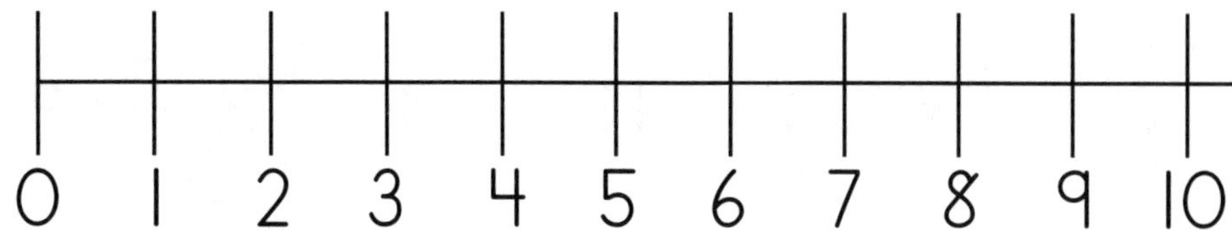

3. 10 – 8 = ____

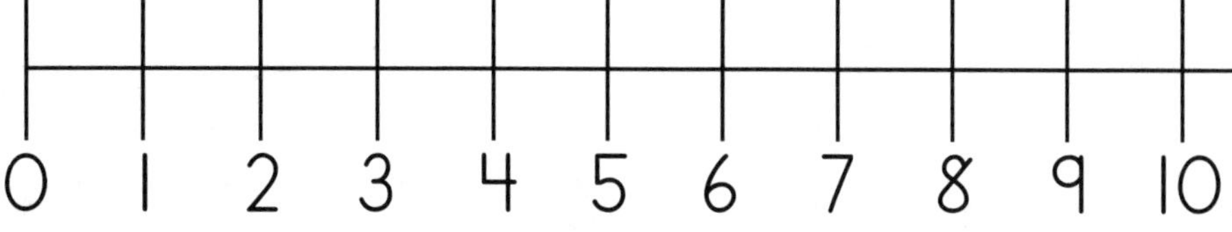

4. 7 – 2 = ____

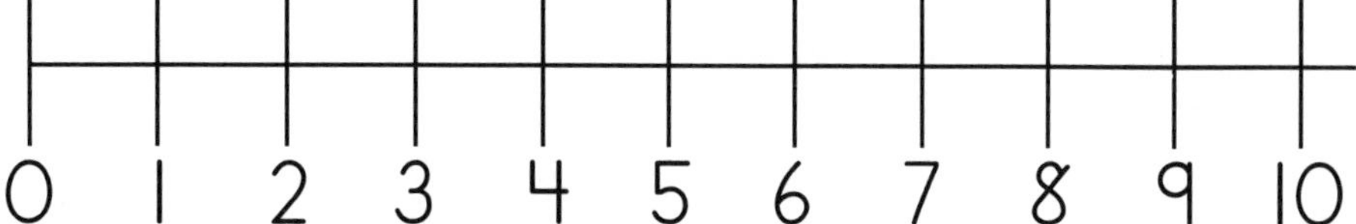

5. 9 – 6 = ____

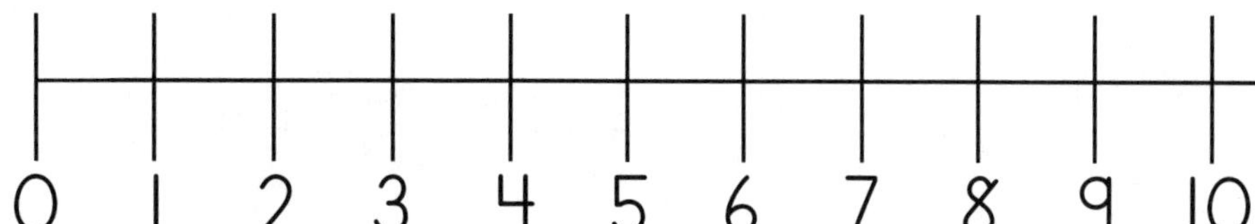

Total Problems: **Total Correct:** **Score:**

Name ____________________

Study the box below. Solve each problem and write the answer in the space below it .

Rule:	**Example:**	**Think to Yourself:**
When subtracting, start with the greater number and count back to the lesser number to find the answer.	10 − 7 3	Start with 10. Count back to 7. 7 8 9 (10)

1. 8 − 7 =
2. 10 − 8 =
3. 9 − 2 =
4. 6 − 5 =
5. 10 − 7 =
6. 8 − 5 =
7. 10 − 3 =
8. 9 − 4 =
9. 7 − 4 =
10. 8 − 2 =
11. 9 − 7 =
12. 6 − 3 =
13. 8 − 3 =
14. 9 − 5 =
15. 8 − 4 =
16. 7 − 3 =
17. 9 − 1 =
18. 6 − 2 =
19. 8 − 6 =
20. 5 − 1 =

Total Problems: **Total Correct:** **Score:**

Name ______________________________

Solve each problem and write the answer in the space below it.

1. $13 - 6$
2. $11 - 5$
3. $13 - 4$
4. $12 - 6$
5. $14 - 9$
6. $14 - 8$
7. $15 - 9$
8. $10 - 8$
9. $12 - 5$
10. $15 - 6$
11. $13 - 8$
12. $11 - 8$
13. $13 - 5$
14. $13 - 9$
15. $15 - 7$
16. $11 - 7$
17. $8 - 4$
18. $13 - 7$
19. $12 - 7$
20. $15 - 3$
21. $14 - 5$
22. $12 - 9$
23. $15 - 5$
24. $12 - 8$
25. $13 - 2$

Total Problems: Total Correct: Score:

Name ______________________

Solve each problem and write the answer in the space below it.

1. 17 − 8
2. 12 − 5
3. 15 − 8
4. 20 − 9
5. 10 − 5
6. 13 − 7
7. 11 − 9
8. 13 − 9
9. 14 − 5
10. 17 − 9
11. 10 − 2
12. 18 − 9
13. 16 − 9
14. 8 − 4
15. 18 − 7
16. 15 − 7
17. 14 − 8
18. 17 − 8
19. 12 − 8
20. 15 − 9
21. 19 − 8
22. 15 − 6
23. 17 − 9
24. 13 − 7
25. 15 − 5

Total Problems: Total Correct: Score:

Name ______________________________

Solve each problem and write the answer on the line beside it.

1. 14 − 5 = ____ 2. 16 − 9 = ____ 3. 20 − 10 = ____

4. 18 − 9 = ____ 5. 15 − 7 = ____ 6. 13 − 7 = ____

7. 13 − 8 = ____ 8. 16 − 9 = ____ 9. 18 − 9 = ____

10. 12 − 5 = ____ 11. 11 − 9 = ____ 12. 14 − 9 = ____

13. 14 − 8 = ____ 14. 12 − 9 = ____ 15. 15 − 8 = ____

16. 17 − 8 = ____ 17. 14 − 5 = ____ 18. 10 − 4 = ____

19. 15 − 9 = ____ 20. 16 − 7 = ____ 21. 16 − 8 = ____

22. 13 − 6 = ____ 23. 15 − 6 = ____ 24. 17 − 8 = ____

25. 14 − 7 = ____ 26. 16 − 6 = ____ 27. 14 − 6 = ____

Total Problems:	Total Correct:	Score:

Name ____________________

Study the example below. Then, solve each problem and write the missing number in the box.

Example: 10 − [7] = 3

Think to Yourself: 10 take away 3 equals what number?

1. 18 − □ = 9
2. 15 − □ = 7
3. 10 − □ = 4
4. 13 − □ = 9
5. 8 − □ = 1
6. 12 − □ = 9
7. 16 − □ = 8
8. 13 − □ = 4
9. 14 − □ = 10
10. 16 − □ = 13
11. 14 − □ = 12
12. 16 − □ = 11
13. 8 − □ = 0
14. 12 − □ = 3
15. 11 − □ = 6
16. 14 − □ = 11
17. 10 − □ = 9
18. 17 − □ = 8
19. 19 − □ = 10
20. 17 − □ = 10

Total Problems: **Total Correct:** **Score:**

Name ________________________________

Study the box below. Solve each problem and write the answer in the space below it.

Rule:	Example:
Draw a line between the tens and ones places. Subtract the ones first, then subtract the tens.	8|3 − 2|3 6|0

1.	2.	3.	4.	5.
69 − 30	73 − 22	80 − 60	83 − 30	29 − 24

6.	7.	8.	9.	10.
65 − 34	96 − 90	78 − 52	25 − 23	47 − 17

11.	12.	13.	14.	15.
51 − 50	99 − 28	62 − 10	85 − 50	96 − 50

16.	17.	18.	19.	20.
62 − 21	75 − 31	83 − 52	88 − 11	86 − 35

Total Problems: Total Correct: Score:

Name ______________________

Two-Digit Subtraction without Regrouping

Solve each problem and write the answer in the space below it.

1.	2.	3.	4.	5.
64 − 40	91 − 60	87 − 12	35 − 24	81 − 21

6.	7.	8.	9.	10.
39 − 28	48 − 27	48 − 23	83 − 41	70 − 20

11.	12.	13.	14.	15.
67 − 40	66 − 33	71 − 51	73 − 30	98 − 54

16.	17.	18.	19.	20.
68 − 51	69 − 23	26 − 13	49 − 46	76 − 63

21.	22.	23.	24.	25.
49 − 20	35 − 25	78 − 62	97 − 15	54 − 10

Total Problems: Total Correct: Score:

Name ______________________________

Three-Digit Subtraction without Regrouping

Solve each problem and write the answer in the space below it.

1. 364 − 124	2. 445 − 213	3. 695 − 434	4. 798 − 581
5. 345 − 222	6. 575 − 250	7. 200 − 100	8. 213 − 102
9. 840 − 230	10. 268 − 111	11. 745 − 434	12. 465 − 120
13. 660 − 200	14. 164 − 160	15. 450 − 150	16. 656 − 333
17. 555 − 232	18. 898 − 354	19. 435 − 224	20. 369 − 145
21. 255 − 144	22. 222 − 222	23. 437 − 430	24. 800 − 500

Total Problems: Total Correct: Score:

Name ______________________________

Three-Digit Subtraction without Regrouping

Solve each problem and write the answer in the space below it.

1. 658 − 250	2. 465 − 335	3. 852 − 441	4. 555 − 340
5. 425 − 120	6. 975 − 525	7. 645 − 521	8. 457 − 321
9. 499 − 311	10. 636 − 212	11. 690 − 540	12. 541 − 240
13. 473 − 123	14. 468 − 357	15. 466 − 155	16. 322 − 100
17. 741 − 140	18. 580 − 270	19. 900 − 300	20. 487 − 250
21. 669 − 558	22. 482 − 360	23. 485 − 150	24. 749 − 600

Total Problems: Total Correct: Score:

Name ________________________________

Use counters to find the answer. Write the answer on the line.

1. Sam has 3 balloons. Then, 2 of the balloons popped. How many balloons does he have now?

   3 − 2 = ____

2. There are 10 birds. 5 fly away. How many birds are left?

   10 − 5 = ____

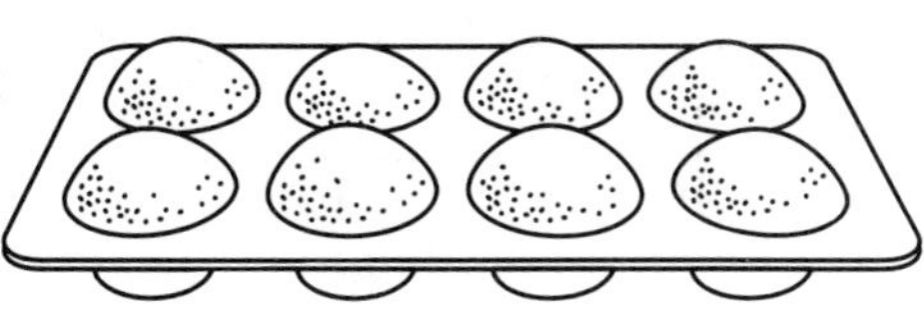

3. Miss Smith bakes 8 muffins. She sells 5. How many muffins does she have left?

   8 − 5 = ____

4. Rob has 6 flowers. He gives 4 flowers to Betty. How many flowers does he have left?

   6 − 4 = ____

Total Problems:	Total Correct:	Score:

Name ______________________

Study the box below. Add or subtract to find each fact family. Write the answer on the lines beside it.

Rule: Select two numbers and write their addition number sentences. Use the answer and write the subtraction number sentences using the first two numbers. The group of number sentences is the **fact family**.	**Example:** 2, 3, 5 2 + 3 = 5 5 − 3 = 2 3 + 2 = 5 5 − 2 = 3

1. 3, 4, 7

   4 + 3 = ____
   3 + 4 = ____
   7 − 4 = ____
   7 − 3 = ____

2. 5, 6, 11

   5 + 6 = ____
   6 + 5 = ____
   11 − 6 = ____
   11 − 5 = ____

3. 7, 8, 15

   7 + 8 = ____
   8 + 7 = ____
   15 − 8 = ____
   15 − 7 = ____

4. 10, 11, 21

   10 + 11 = ____
   11 + 10 = ____
   21 − 11 = ____
   21 − 10 = ____

5. 6, 7, 13

   6 + 7 = ____
   7 + 6 = ____
   13 − 7 = ____
   13 − 6 = ____

6. 8, 9, 17

   8 + 9 = ____
   9 + 8 = ____
   17 − 9 = ____
   17 − 8 = ____

Total Problems: Total Correct: Score:

Name ______________________________

Two-Digit Mixed Practice without Regrouping

Add or subtract each problem. Write the answer in the space below it.

1. $\begin{array}{r} 88 \\ -11 \\ \hline \end{array}$
2. $\begin{array}{r} 72 \\ +13 \\ \hline \end{array}$
3. $\begin{array}{r} 85 \\ -42 \\ \hline \end{array}$
4. $\begin{array}{r} 54 \\ +40 \\ \hline \end{array}$
5. $\begin{array}{r} 48 \\ -38 \\ \hline \end{array}$
6. $\begin{array}{r} 12 \\ +42 \\ \hline \end{array}$
7. $\begin{array}{r} 65 \\ -41 \\ \hline \end{array}$
8. $\begin{array}{r} 87 \\ +12 \\ \hline \end{array}$
9. $\begin{array}{r} 65 \\ -42 \\ \hline \end{array}$
10. $\begin{array}{r} 50 \\ +31 \\ \hline \end{array}$
11. $\begin{array}{r} 96 \\ -23 \\ \hline \end{array}$
12. $\begin{array}{r} 23 \\ +63 \\ \hline \end{array}$
13. $\begin{array}{r} 78 \\ -35 \\ \hline \end{array}$
14. $\begin{array}{r} 32 \\ +57 \\ \hline \end{array}$
15. $\begin{array}{r} 74 \\ -52 \\ \hline \end{array}$
16. $\begin{array}{r} 73 \\ -22 \\ \hline \end{array}$
17. $\begin{array}{r} 78 \\ -62 \\ \hline \end{array}$
18. $\begin{array}{r} 11 \\ +73 \\ \hline \end{array}$
19. $\begin{array}{r} 64 \\ -23 \\ \hline \end{array}$
20. $\begin{array}{r} 60 \\ +20 \\ \hline \end{array}$
21. $\begin{array}{r} 86 \\ -82 \\ \hline \end{array}$
22. $\begin{array}{r} 85 \\ -82 \\ \hline \end{array}$
23. $\begin{array}{r} 85 \\ +13 \\ \hline \end{array}$
24. $\begin{array}{r} 88 \\ -10 \\ \hline \end{array}$
25. $\begin{array}{r} 54 \\ +24 \\ \hline \end{array}$

Total Problems: **Total Correct:** **Score:**

Name ______________________________

Two-Digit Mixed Practice without Regrouping

Add or subtract each problem. Write the answer in the space below it.

1. 30 + 25	2. 63 − 41	3. 50 + 38	4. 46 − 23	5. 73 + 26
6. 54 − 42	7. 61 + 23	8. 75 − 55	9. 20 + 40	10. 18 + 10
11. 91 − 60	12. 21 + 71	13. 82 − 52	14. 48 − 23	15. 36 + 22
16. 95 − 30	17. 80 + 19	18. 23 + 23	19. 86 − 21	20. 45 + 20
21. 76 − 16	22. 49 − 32	23. 13 + 13	24. 54 − 10	25. 35 + 10

Total Problems: Total Correct: Score:

Name ______________________________

Study the examples below.

Look at the triangle. It is divided into 2 equal parts. One part is shaded, and the other part is not. $\frac{1}{2}$ of the triangle is shaded.

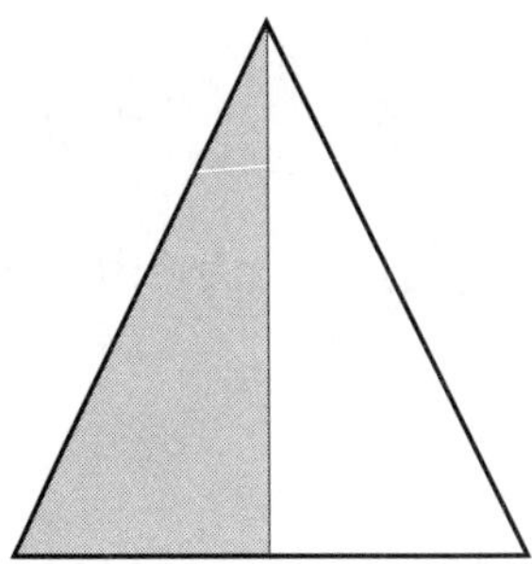

Look at the circle. It is divided into 2 equal parts. One part is shaded, and the other part is not. $\frac{1}{2}$ of the circle is shaded.

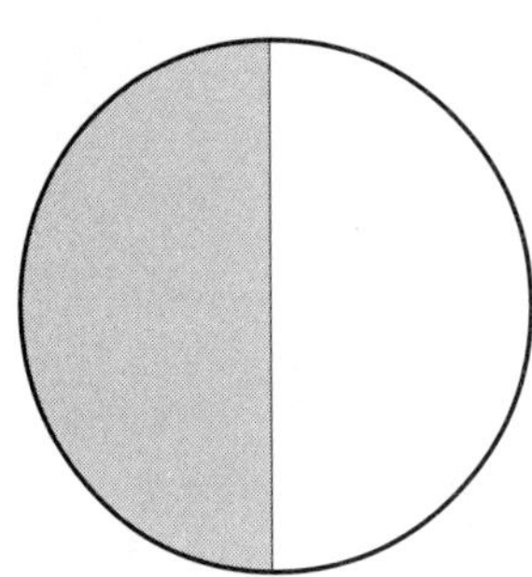

Look at the square. It is divided into 4 equal parts. One part is shaded, and the others are not. $\frac{1}{4}$ of the square is shaded.

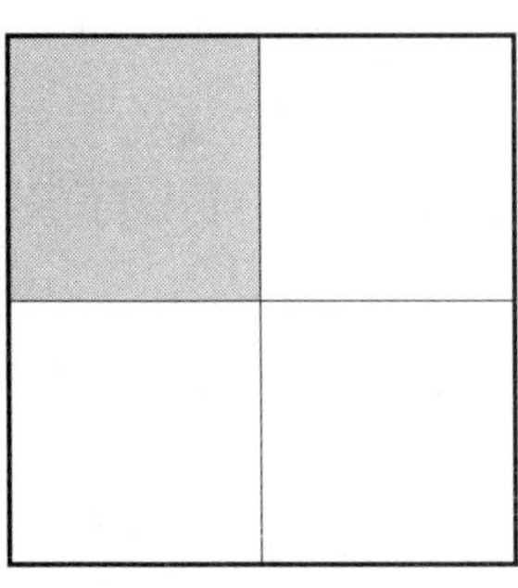

Look at the rectangle. It is divided into 4 equal parts. One part is shaded, and the others are not. $\frac{1}{4}$ of the rectangle is shaded.

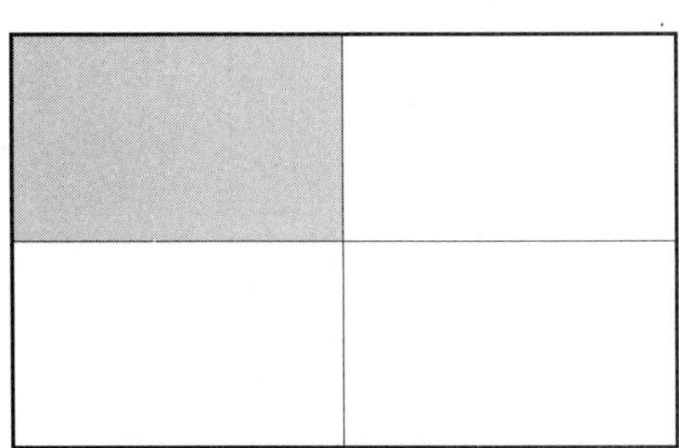

Name ______________________________

Follow the directions in each problem.

1. Color $\frac{1}{2}$ red.
   Color $\frac{1}{2}$ yellow.

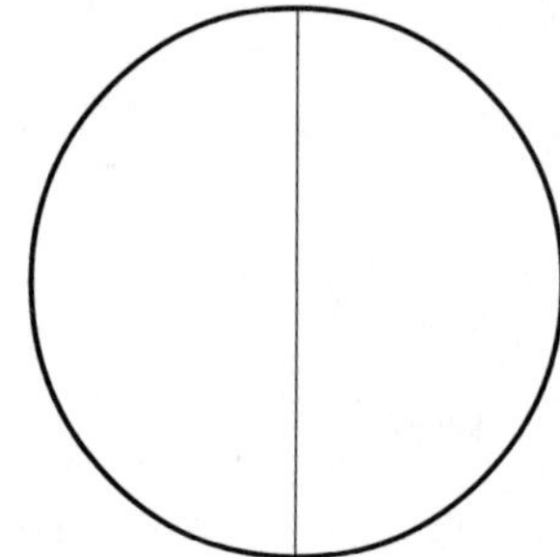

2. Color $\frac{1}{2}$ blue.
   Color $\frac{1}{2}$ green.

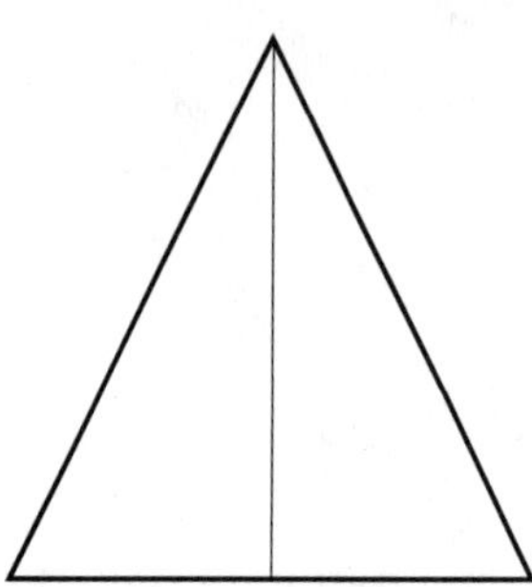

3. Color $\frac{1}{2}$ black.
   Color $\frac{1}{2}$ brown.

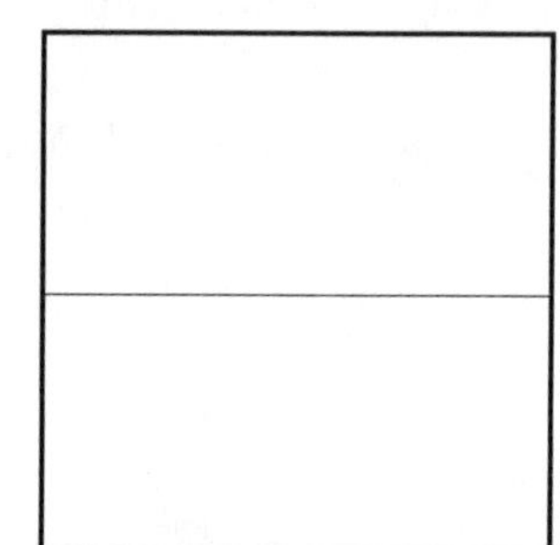

4. Color $\frac{1}{4}$ purple.
   Color $\frac{1}{4}$ orange.

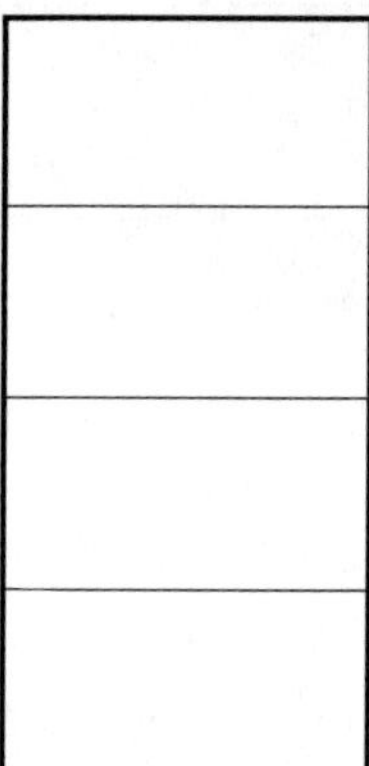

5. Color $\frac{1}{4}$ green.
   Color $\frac{1}{4}$ red.

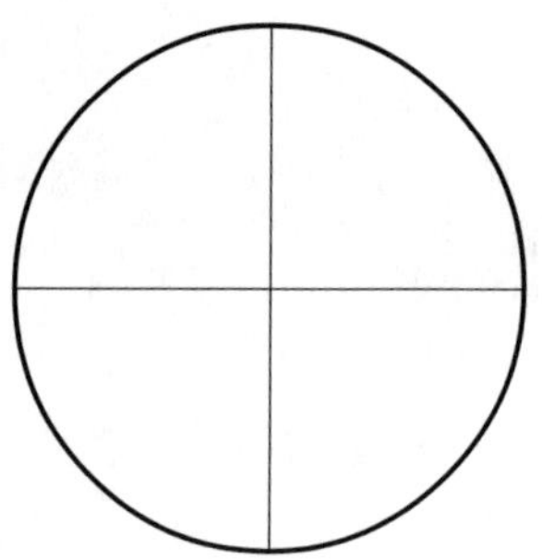

6. Color $\frac{1}{4}$ yellow.
   Color $\frac{1}{4}$ blue.

Total Problems: Total Correct: Score:

Name ______________________________

Answer the word problems. Color the parts of each pizza to help solve the problems. Write the answer on the lines below.

1. Sam and Sarah each bought a cheese pizza for dinner. Sam cut his pizza into fourths. Sarah cut her pizza in half. If Sam ate $\frac{3}{4}$ of his pizza and Sarah ate $\frac{1}{2}$ of her pizza, who ate more pizza?

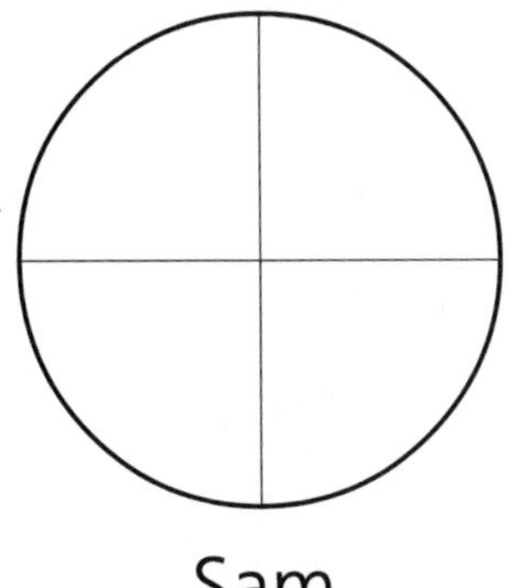

Sam

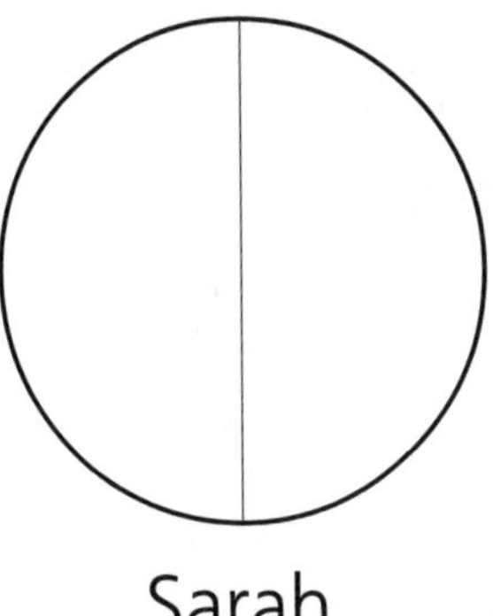

Sarah

__________________ ate more pizza.

2. Nicole and Paul ate pizza for lunch. Nicole ate $\frac{1}{4}$ of her pizza. Paul ate $\frac{1}{2}$ of his pizza. Who ate more pizza?

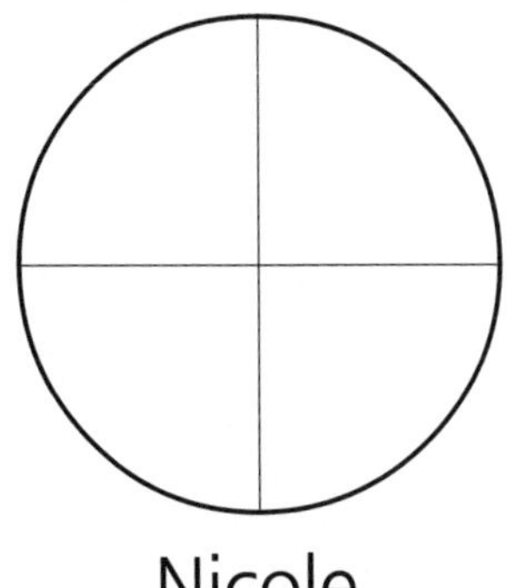

Nicole

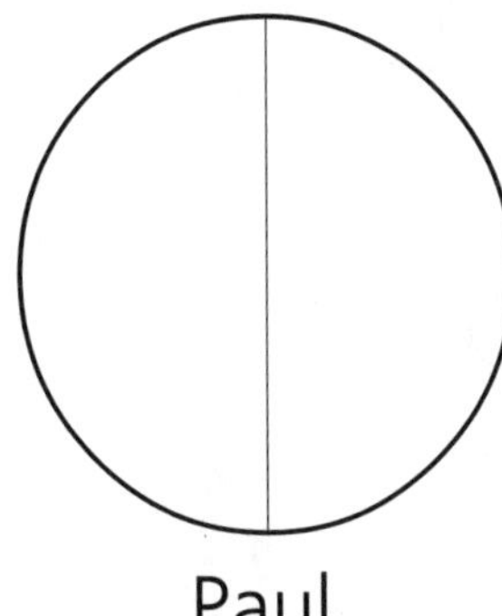

Paul

__________________ ate more pizza.

Total Problems:	Total Correct:	Score:

Name ______________________

Study the box below. Draw the clock hands on each clock to match the time shown.

Rule:	**Example:**
The hour hand is shorter than the minute hand.	2:00 

1. 1:00

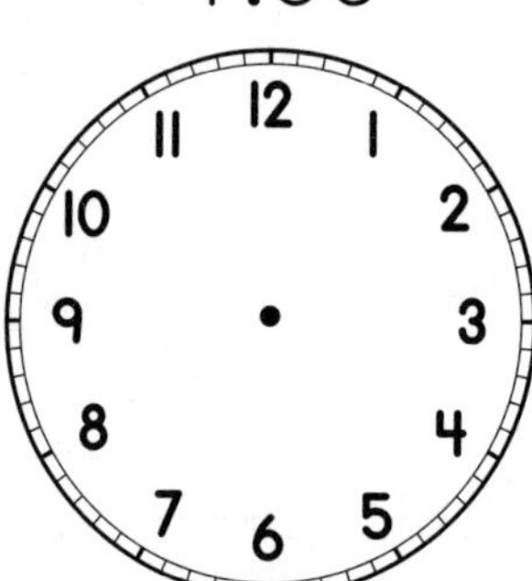

2. 5:00

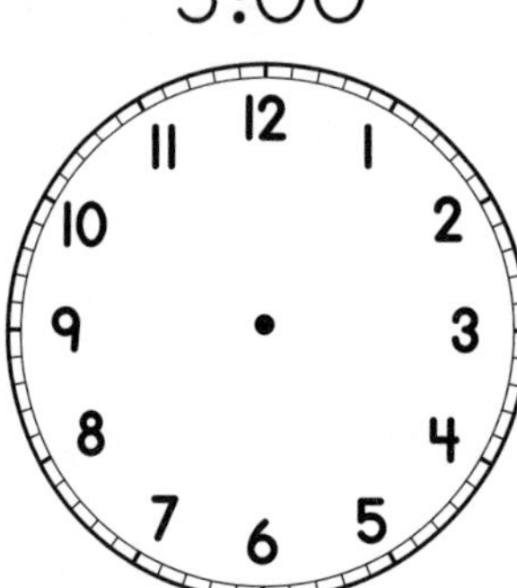

3. 9:00

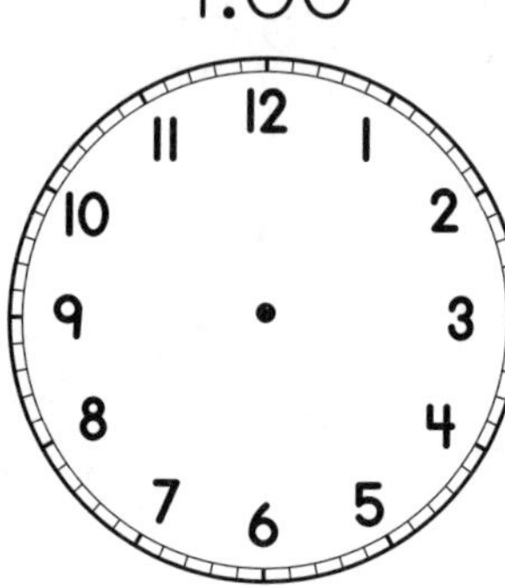

4. 4:00

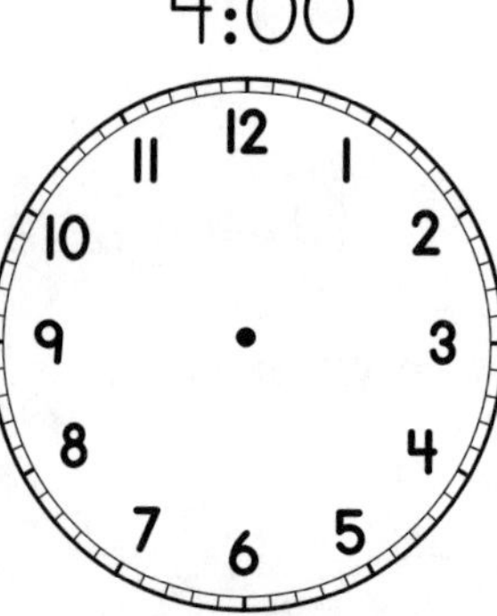

5. 6:00

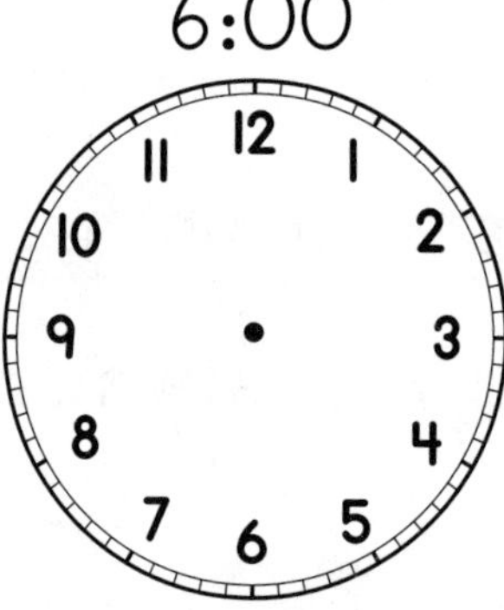

6. 10:00

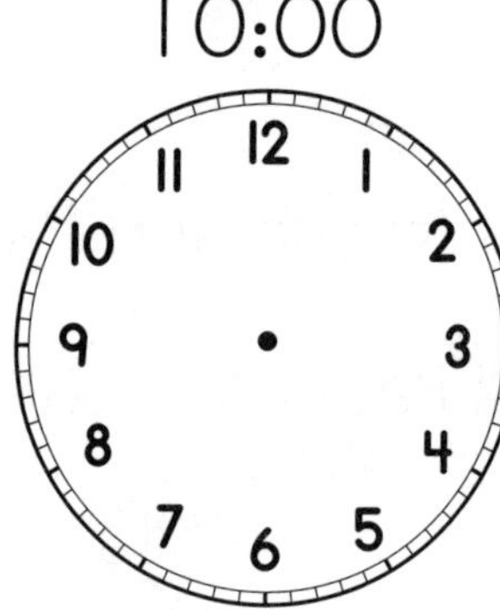

7. 3:00

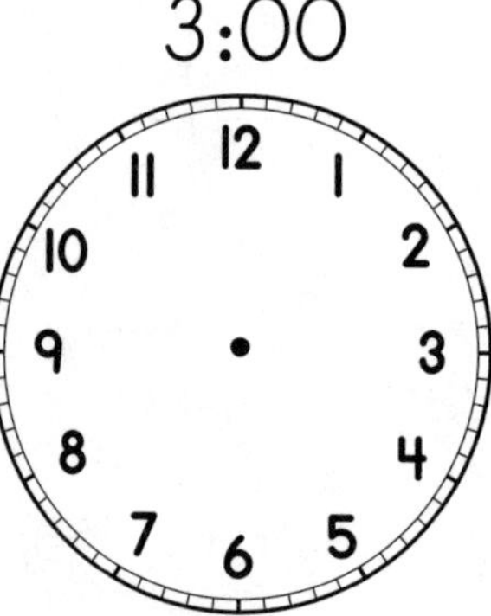

8. 11:00

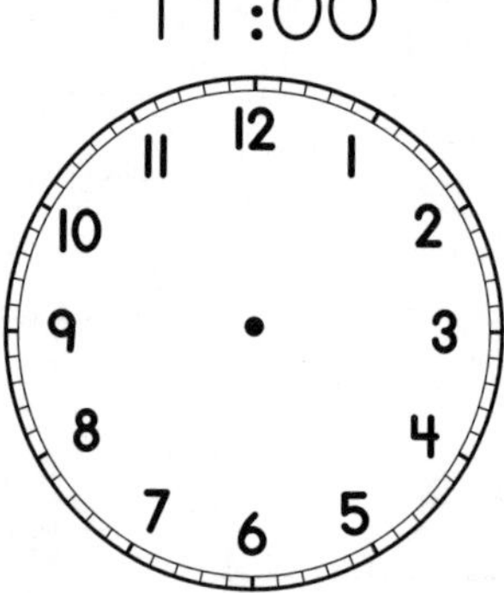

9. 8:00

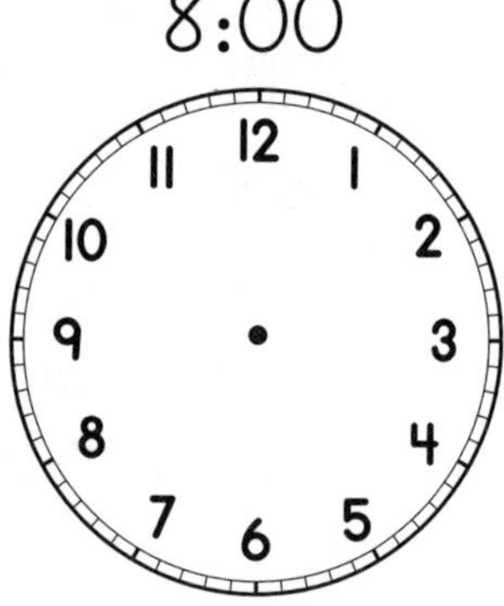

Total Problems: **Total Correct:** **Score:**

Name ______________________________

Study the example below. Write each time on the line provided. Draw the clock hands to match each time.

Example:

It is 4 o'clock.

In one hour it will be 5 o'clock.

1. It is 2 o'clock.

In one hour it will be ______ o'clock.

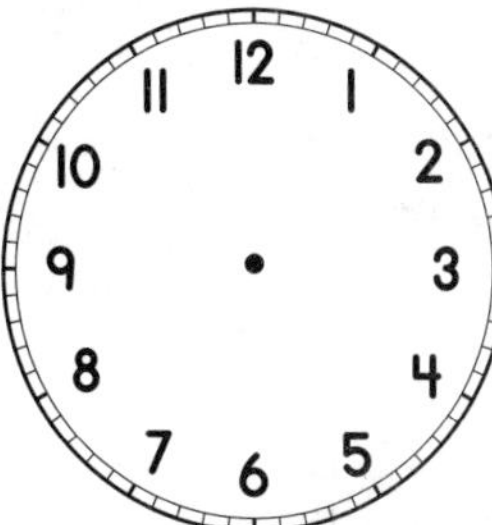

2. It is 8 o'clock.

In one hour it will be ______ o'clock.

3. It is 10 o'clock.

In one hour it will be ______ o'clock.

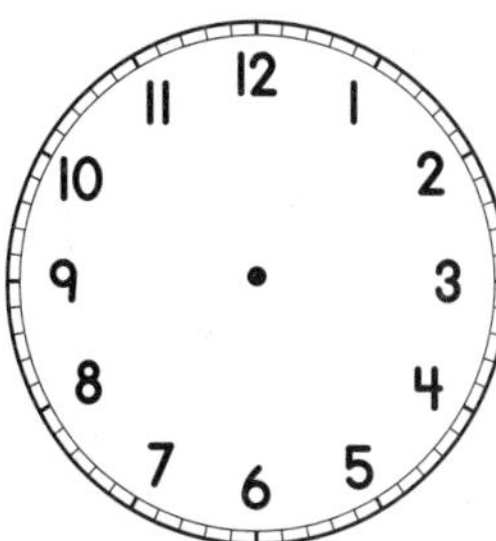

4. It is 12 o'clock.

In one hour it will be ______ o'clock.

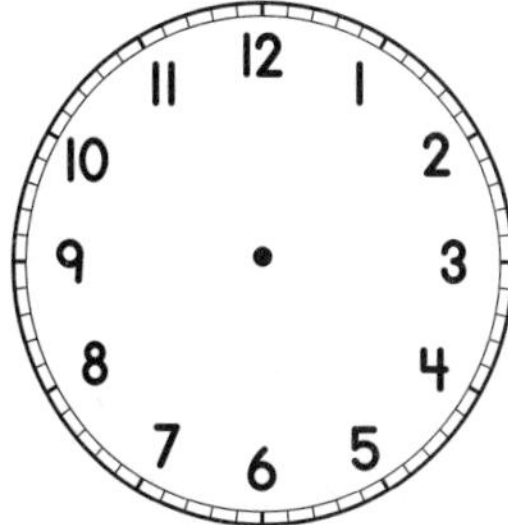

Total Problems: **Total Correct:** **Score:**

Name ______________________________

Study the example below. Write each time on the lines provided. Draw the clock hands to match each time.

Example:

It is 3 o'clock.

One hour earlier it was __2__ o'clock.

1. It is ____ o'clock.

One hour earlier it was ____ o'clock.

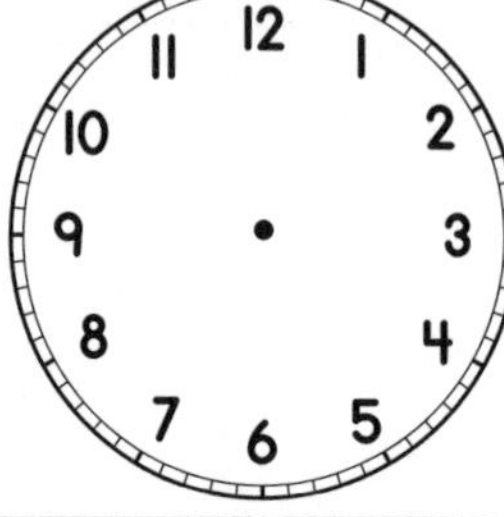

2. It is ____ o'clock.

One hour earlier it was ____ o'clock.

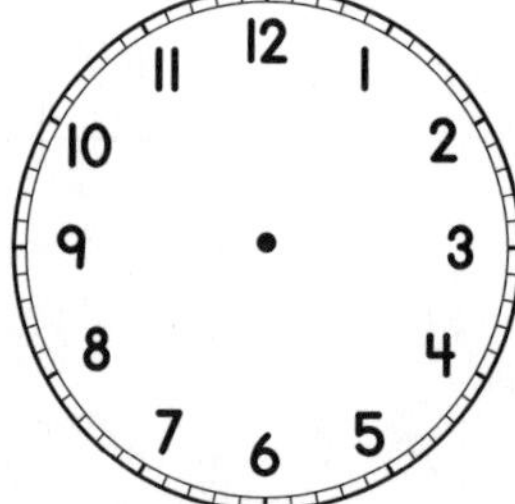

3. It is ____ o'clock.

One hour earlier it was ____ o'clock.

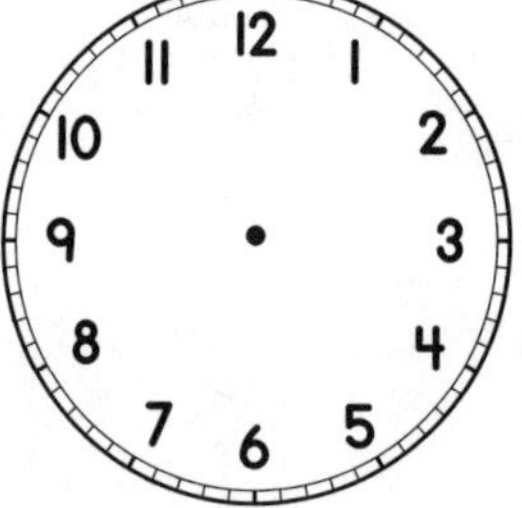

4. It is ____ o'clock.

One hour earlier it was ____ o'clock.

Total Problems: **Total Correct:** **Score:**

Name ______________________

Study the box below. On the lines provided, write where the clock hands point. Then, write each time.

Example:

The hour hand is between the __2__ and __3__.
The minute hand points to the __6__.
It is __2:30__.

1.

The hour hand is between the _____ and the _____.
The minute hand points to the _____.
It is ___________.

2.

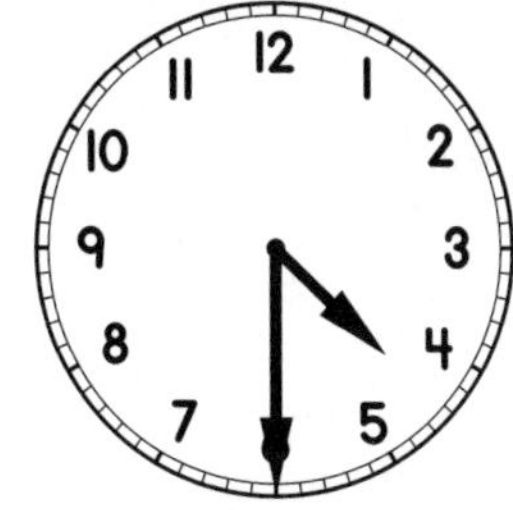

The hour hand is between the _____ and the _____.
The minute hand points to the _____.
It is ___________.

3.

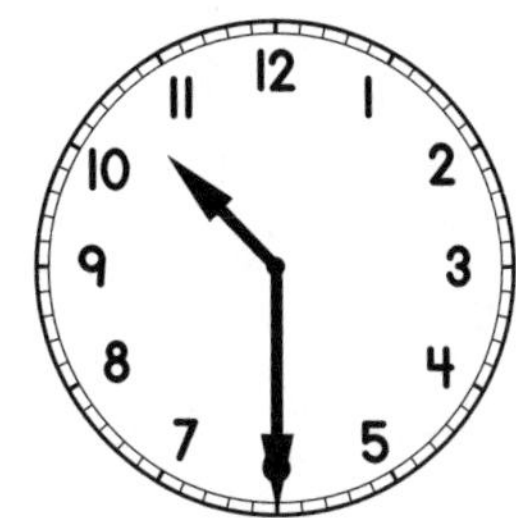

The hour hand is between the _____ and the _____.
The minute hand points to the _____.
It is ___________.

4.

The hour hand is between the _____ and the _____.
The minute hand points to the _____.
It is ___________.

Total Problems: **Total Correct:** **Score:**

Name ______________________

Write each time on the line provided.

1. 
______

2. 
______

3. 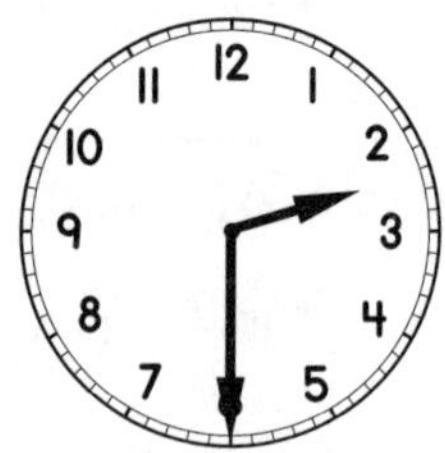
______

4. 
______

5. 
______

6. 
______

7. 
______

8. 
______

9. 
______

10. 
______

11. 
______

12. 
______

13. 
______

14. 
______

15. 
______

Total Problems: Total Correct: Score:

Name ________________________________

Time to the Hour and Half-Hour

Draw a line from each clock to the correct time.

1. 

2:00

6:30

2. 

3. 

2:30

8:00

4. 

5. 

9:30

7:00

6. 

7. 

4:30

1:30

8. 

9. 

12:00

11:30

10. 

Total Problems:	Total Correct:	Score:

Name ______________________________

Solve each word problem. Draw the hands on the clock. Write each time on the line provided.

1. Sam starts his homework at 3:00. It takes him a half-hour. What time does he finish?

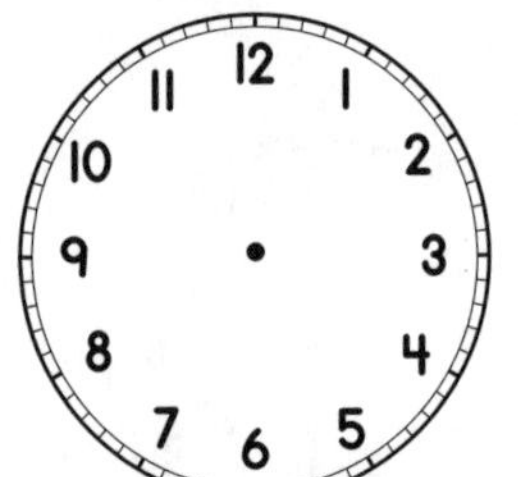

____

2. Lisa goes to lunch at 12:00. She eats for 1 hour. What time does Lisa finish lunch?

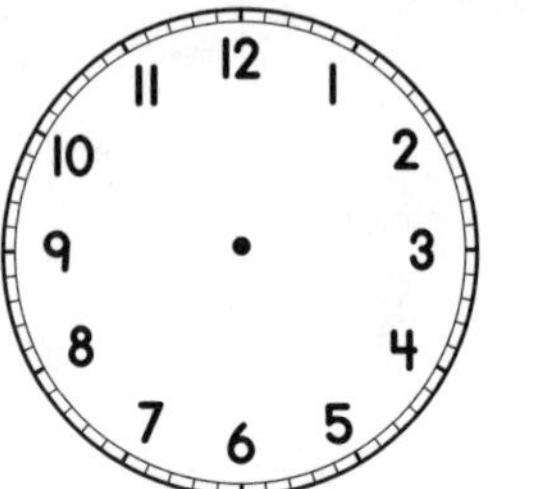

____

3. Kevin walks his dog at 7:00. He walks his dog for a half-hour. What time does he finish walking his dog?

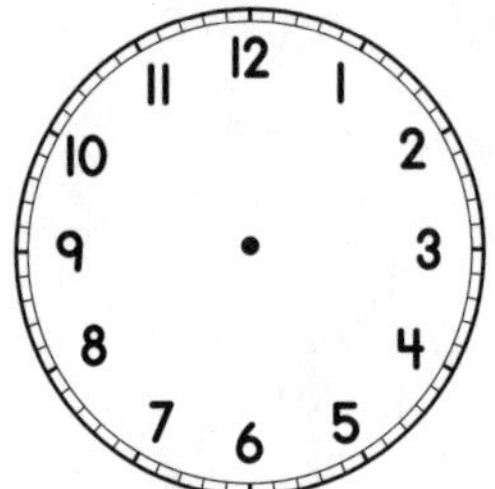

____

4. Chris watches his favorite television show at 8:30. It lasts for 1 hour. What time does Chris finish watching this show?

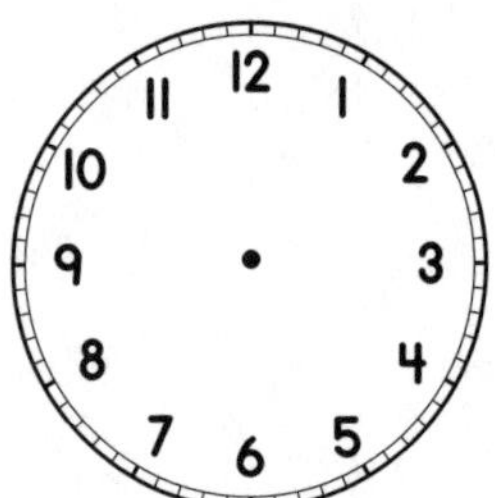

____

5. Alex reads his book at 8:00. He reads for 1 hour. What time does he finish?

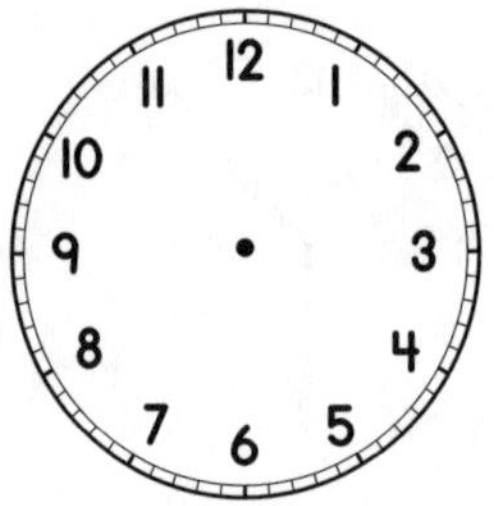

____

6. Kacey washes dishes at 6:30. It takes her a half-hour. What time does she finish?

____

Total Problems:	Total Correct:	Score:

Name ______________________

Solve each word problem. Draw the hands on the clock. Write each time on the line provided.

1. Kate walks to school at 7:30. It takes her a half-hour. What time does she get to school?

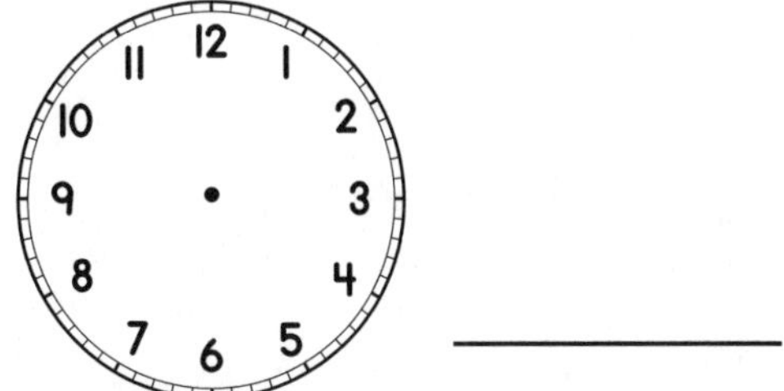

2. Will mows the grass at 6:00. It takes him 1 hour to finish. What time does he finish?

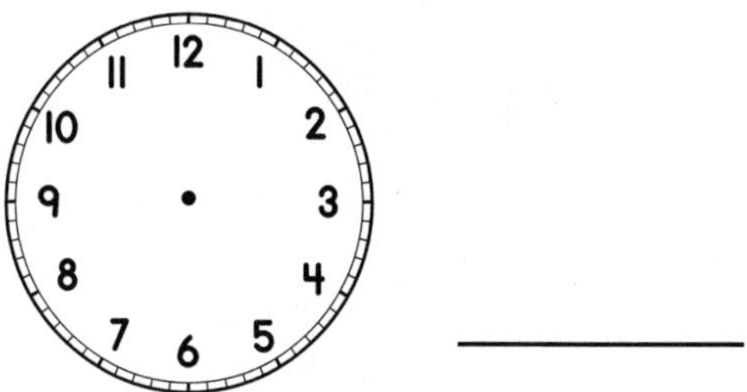

3. Susan bakes cookies at 2:00. It takes her a half-hour. What time do the cookies finish?

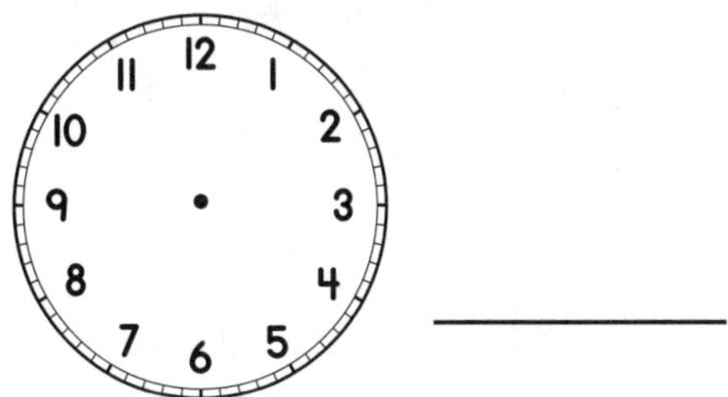

4. Tyler sweeps the floor at 12:00. It takes him a half-hour. What time does he finish?

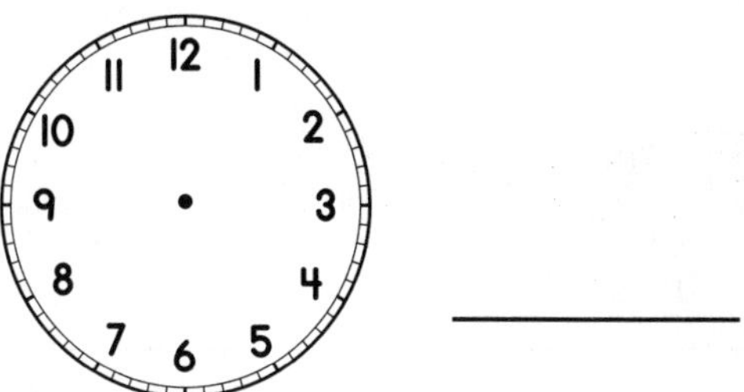

5. Wendy watches a movie at 5:00. The movie lasts for 2 hours. What time does the movie finish?

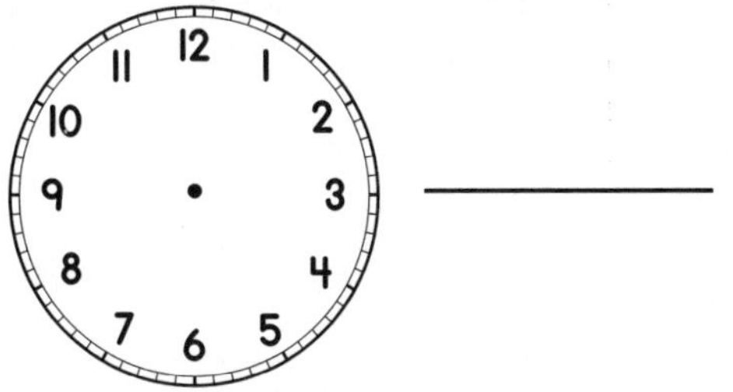

6. Ken writes a story at 9:30. It takes him a half-hour. What time does he finish?

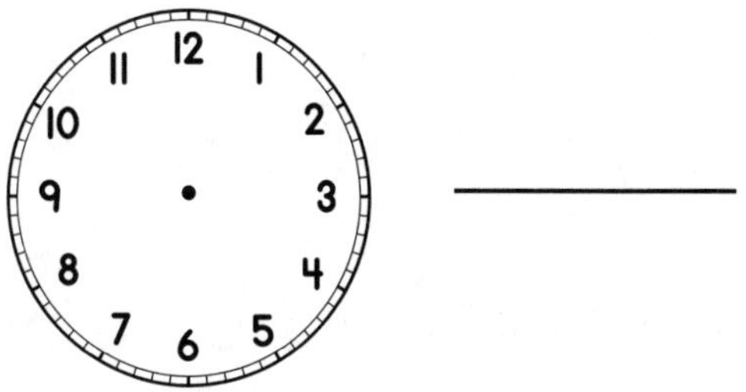

Total Problems: **Total Correct:** **Score:**

Name ____________________

Fill in the calendar dates. Then, answer the questions on the lines provided. This month has 31 days. The first day of the month is Monday.

January

Sunday	Monday	Tuesday	Wednesday	Thursday	Friday	Saturday

1. How many Wednesdays are in January? ____________________
2. What day of the week is January 13? ____________________
3. How many Fridays are in January? ____________________
4. What day of the week is January 31? ____________________
5. How many Tuesdays are in January? ____________________

Total Problems: **Total Correct:** **Score:**

Name ______________________________

Fill in the calendar dates. Then, answer the questions on the lines provided. This month has 30 days. The first day of the month is Wednesday.

April

Sunday	Monday	Tuesday	Wednesday	Thursday	Friday	Saturday

1. How many Fridays are in April? ______________________________
2. What day of the week is April 7? ______________________________
3. How many Mondays are in April? ______________________________
4. Write the dates of the Mondays in April. ______________________
5. What day of the week is April 10? ______________________________

Total Problems: **Total Correct:** **Score:**

Fill in the calendar dates. Then, answer the questions on the lines provided. This month has 31 days. The first day of the month is Monday.

December

Sunday	Monday	Tuesday	Wednesday	Thursday	Friday	Saturday

1. What day of the week is December 4? ____________________
2. How many Wednesdays are in December? ____________________
3. What day of the week is December 20? ____________________
4. How many Fridays are in December? ____________________
5. What day of the week is December 31? ____________________

Total Problems: Total Correct: Score:

Name ______________________________

Study the rule below. Then, count each group of coins. Write the amount on the line beside it.

Rule:

A penny equals 1 cent.
1¢

A nickel equals 5 cents.
5¢

1.     ________¢

2.      ________¢

3.   ________¢

4.    ________¢

5.           ________¢

Total Problems: **Total Correct:** **Score:**

Name ______________________

Count each group of coins. Write the amount on the line beside it.

1.  

______ ¢

2.    

______ ¢

3.  

______ ¢

4.  

______ ¢

5. 

______ ¢

6.     

______ ¢

7.  

______ ¢

8.    

______ ¢

Total Problems: Total Correct: Score:

Name ______________________________

Study the rule below. Then, count each group of coins. Write the amount on the line beside it.

Rule:

A dime equals 10 cents.

10¢

1.      ________¢

2.       ________¢

3.      ________¢

4.      ________¢

5.     ________¢

Total Problems: **Total Correct:** **Score:**

Name ______________________________ **Dimes and Pennies**

Count the coins in each group. Write the amount on the line beside it.

1.   ________¢

2.   ________¢

3.   ________¢

4.      ________¢

5.  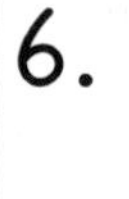  ________¢

6.      ________¢

7.      ________¢

8.     ________¢

Total Problems: **Total Correct:** **Score:**

Name ______________________________

Circle the coins needed to buy each toy.

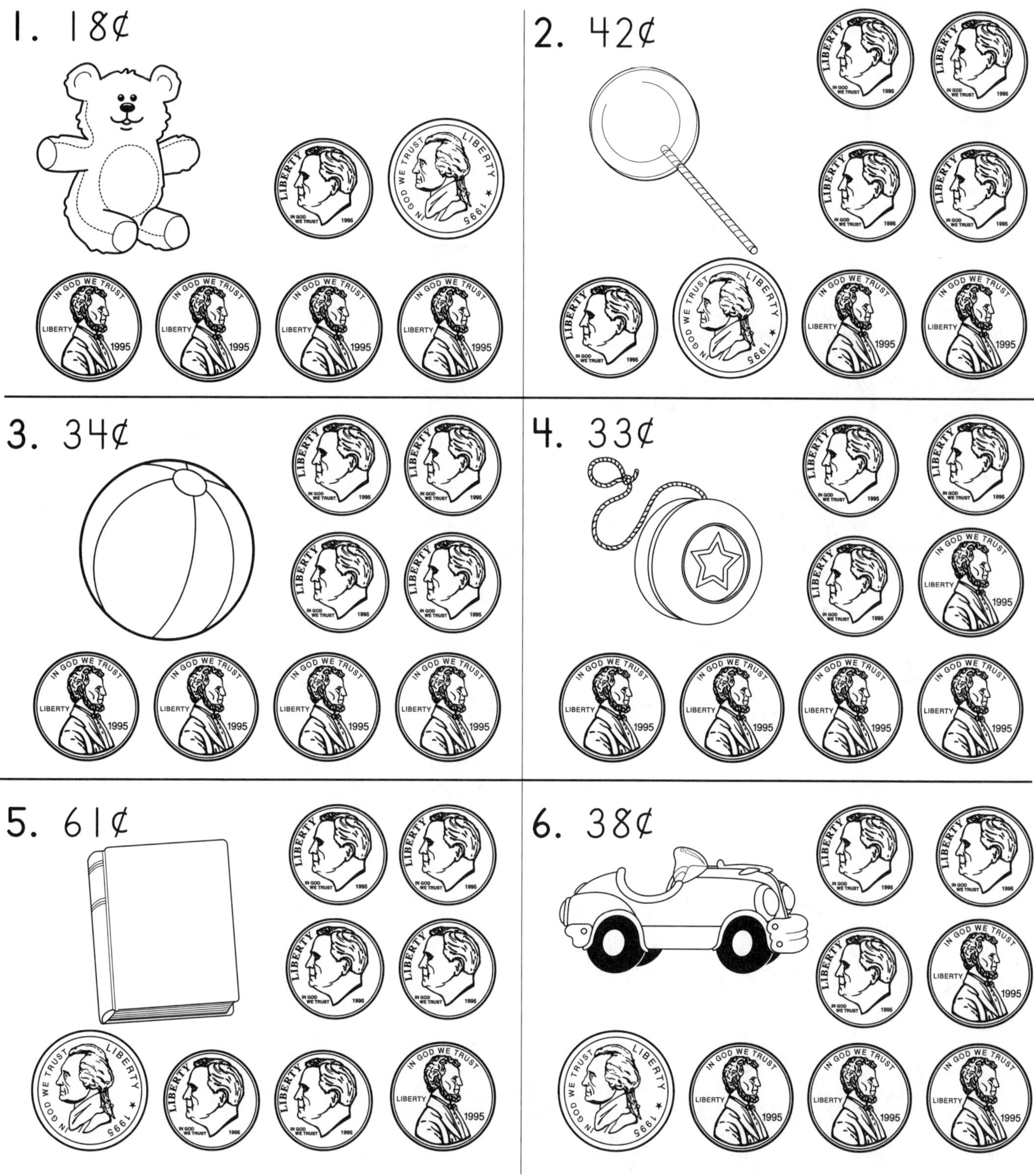

Total Problems: Total Correct: Score:

Name ______________________________

Quarters, Dimes, Nickels, and Pennies

Study the rule below. Then, draw a line from each group of coins to the correct amount.

Rule:

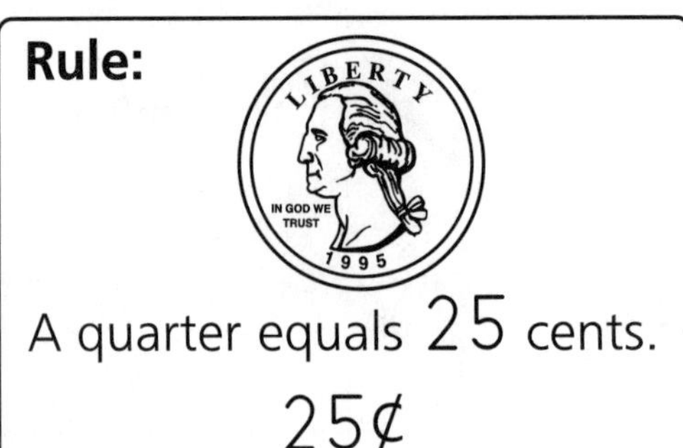

A quarter equals 25 cents.

25¢

1.  65¢

2. 82¢

3. 60¢

4.

32¢

5. 41¢

Total Problems: **Total Correct:** **Score:**

Name ______________________________

Quarters, Dimes, Nickels, and Pennies

Color the coins needed to buy each item.

1\.

51¢

2\.

36¢

3\.

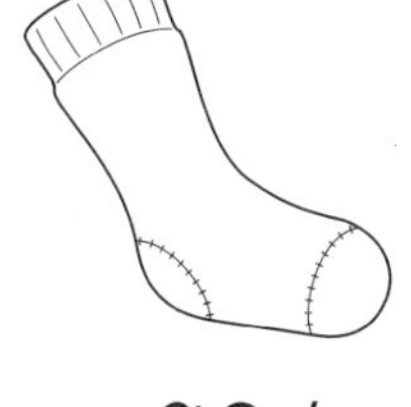

80¢

4\.

41¢

5\.

61¢

Total Problems:	**Total Correct:**	**Score:**

Name ____________________________

Using the pictures below, answer each question on the line beside it.

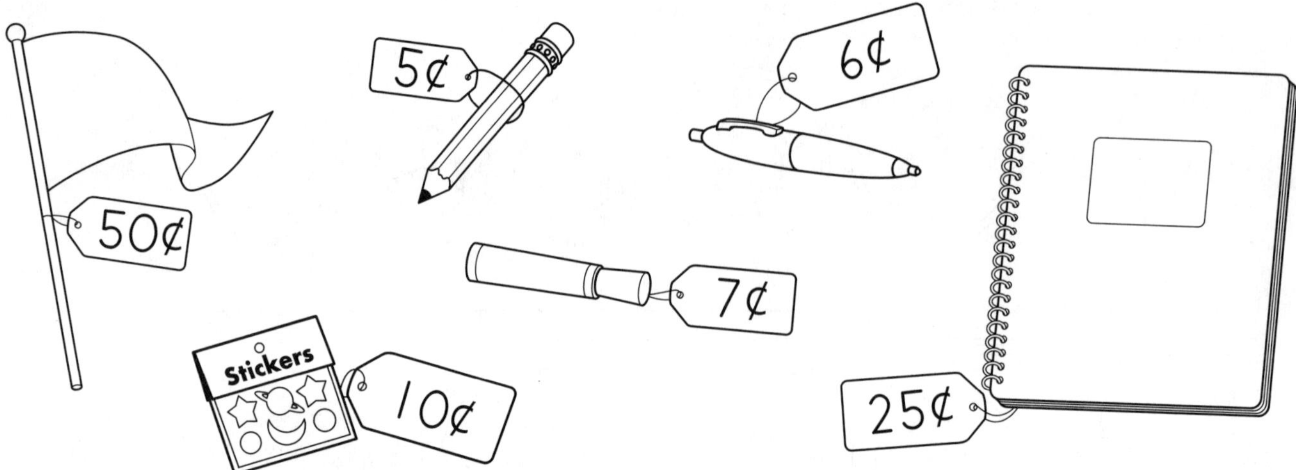

1. Circle 4 things you will buy. Cross out the coins you will need. How much money do you have left? __________¢

2. You have 35¢. You buy a pencil. How much money do you have left? __________¢

3. You have 50¢. You buy a pack of stickers. How much money do you have left? __________¢

Total Problems: Total Correct: Score:

Name ______________________

Study the example below. Then, write the length of each object on the line beside it.

Example:

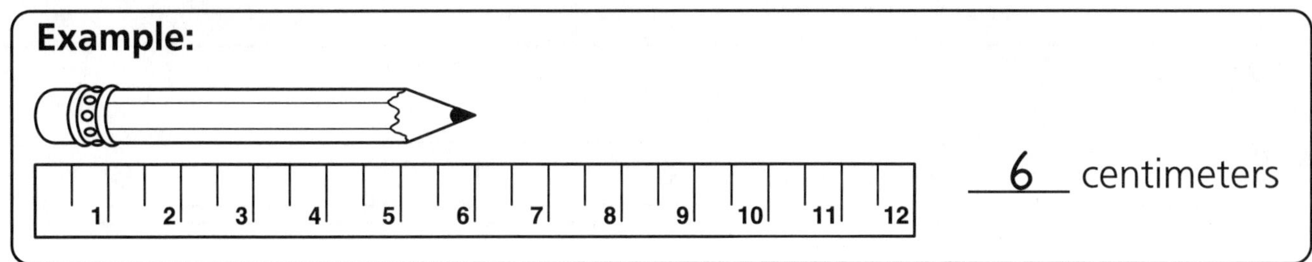

6 centimeters

1.

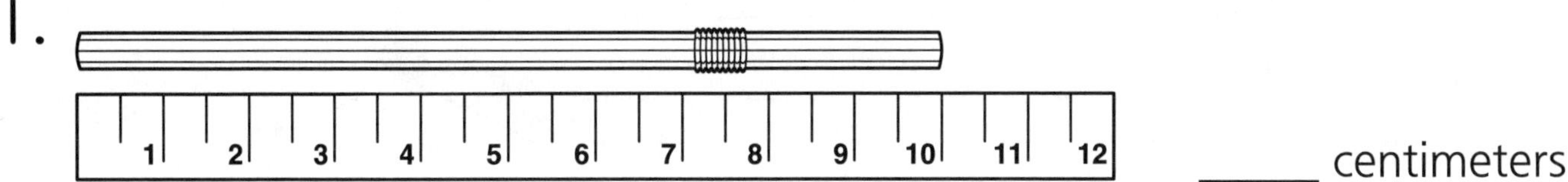

_____ centimeters

2.

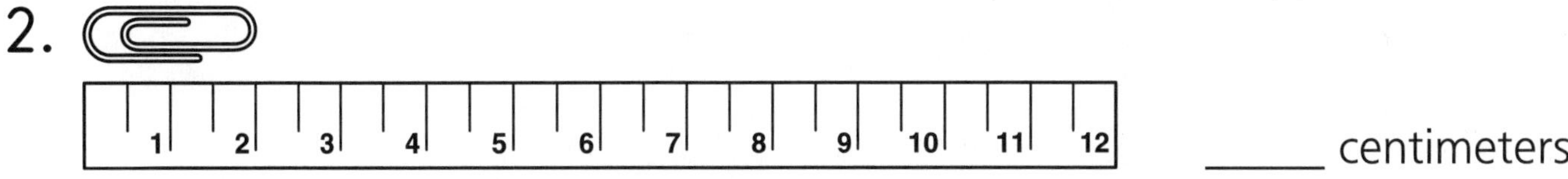

_____ centimeters

3.

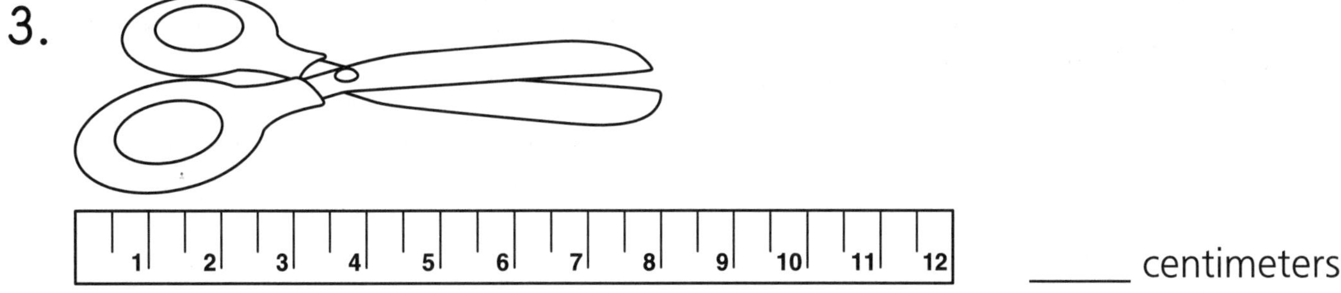

_____ centimeters

4.

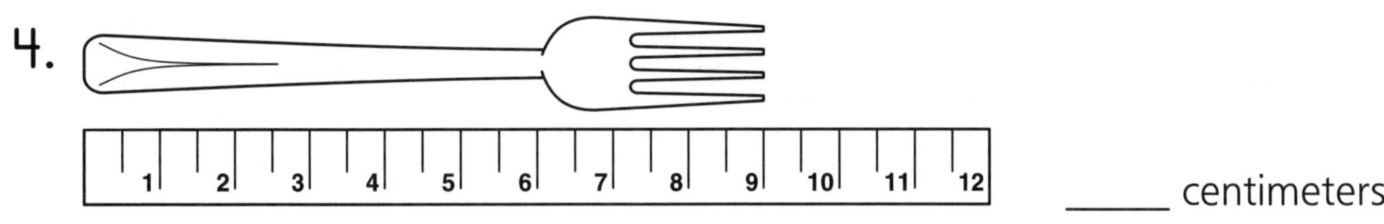

_____ centimeters

5.

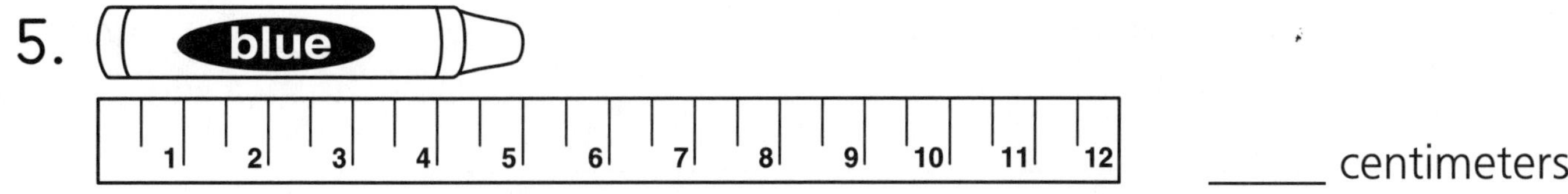

_____ centimeters

Total Problems: **Total Correct:** **Score:**

Name ______________________________

Study the example below. Then, find the length of each object in inches. Write the answer on the line beside it.

Example:

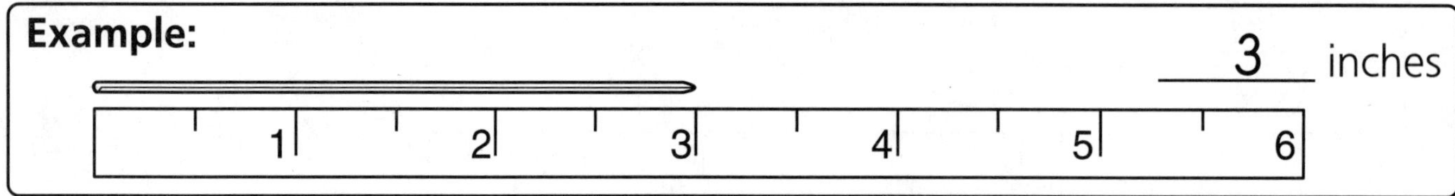

3 inches

1.

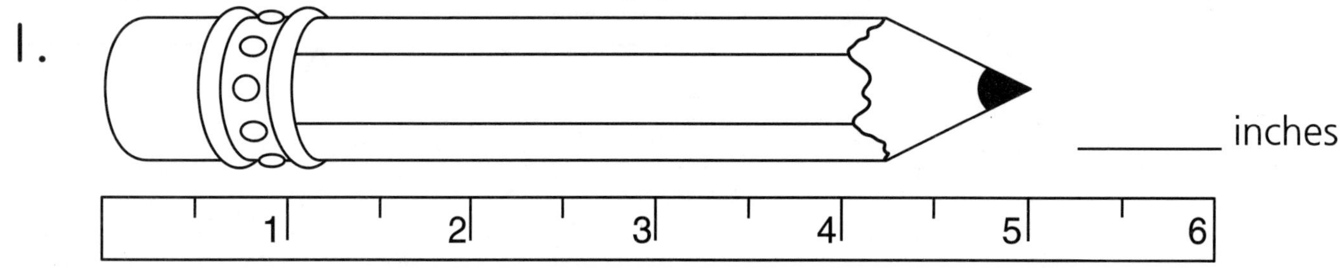

______ inches

2.

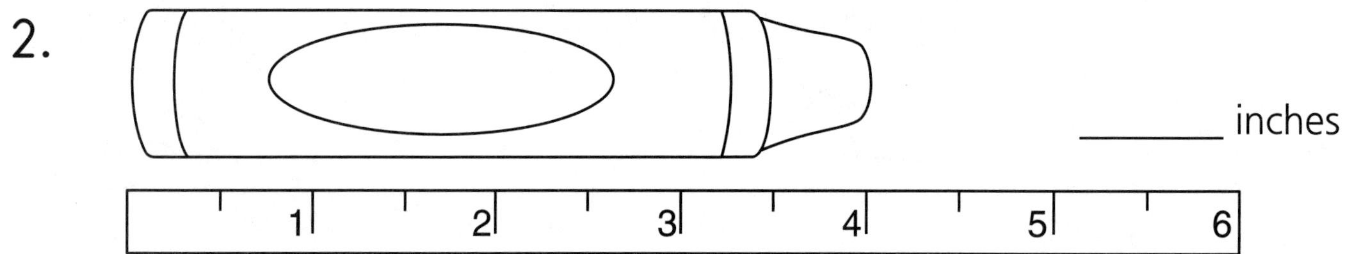

______ inches

3.

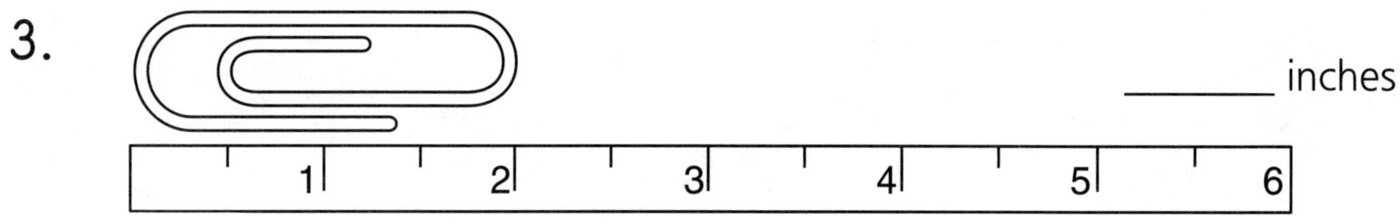

______ inches

4.

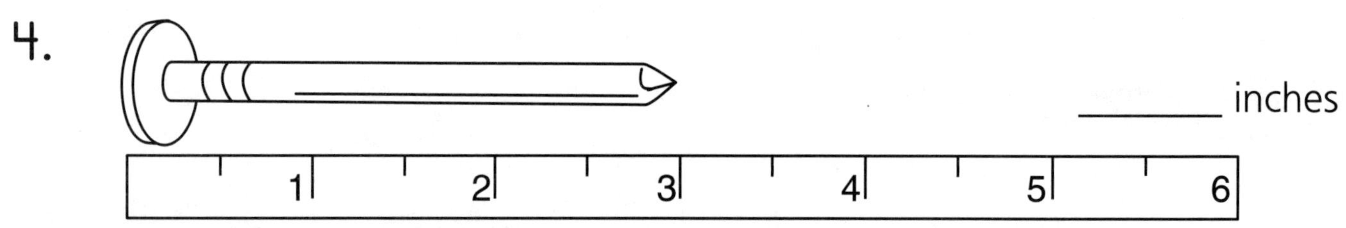

______ inches

Total Problems: **Total Correct:** **Score:**

Name ______________________________

Study the examples below. Then, follow the directions for each problem.

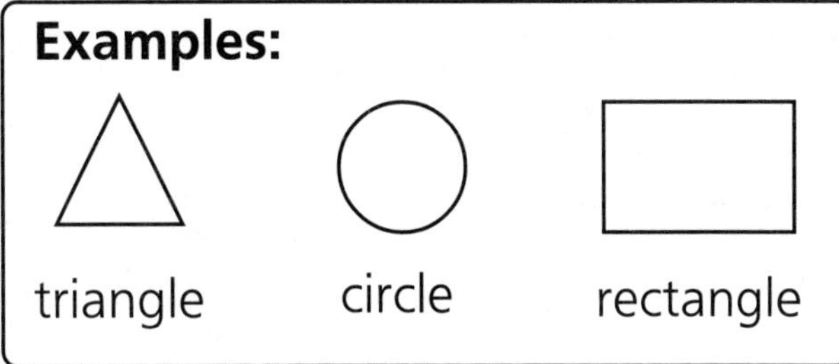

1. Color the triangles red.
   Color the circles blue.
   Color the rectangles green.

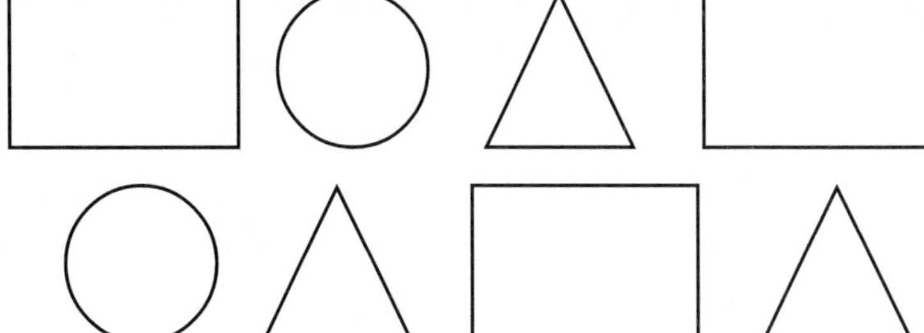

2. Count the shapes above. Write how many of each shape there are on the lines provided.

   _____ triangles _____ circles _____ rectangles

---

3. Color the circles yellow.
   Color the triangles orange.
   Color the rectangles red.

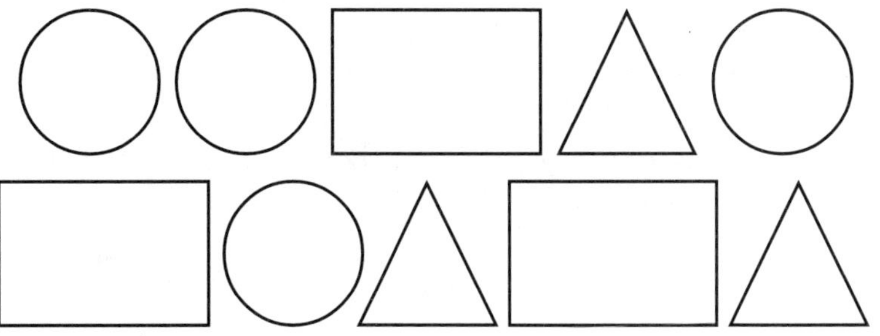

4. Count the shapes above. Write how many of each shape there are on the lines provided.

   _____ triangles _____ circles _____ rectangles

Total Problems:	Total Correct:	Score:

Name ______________________

Study the examples below. Then, in each problem, cross out the shape that does not belong.

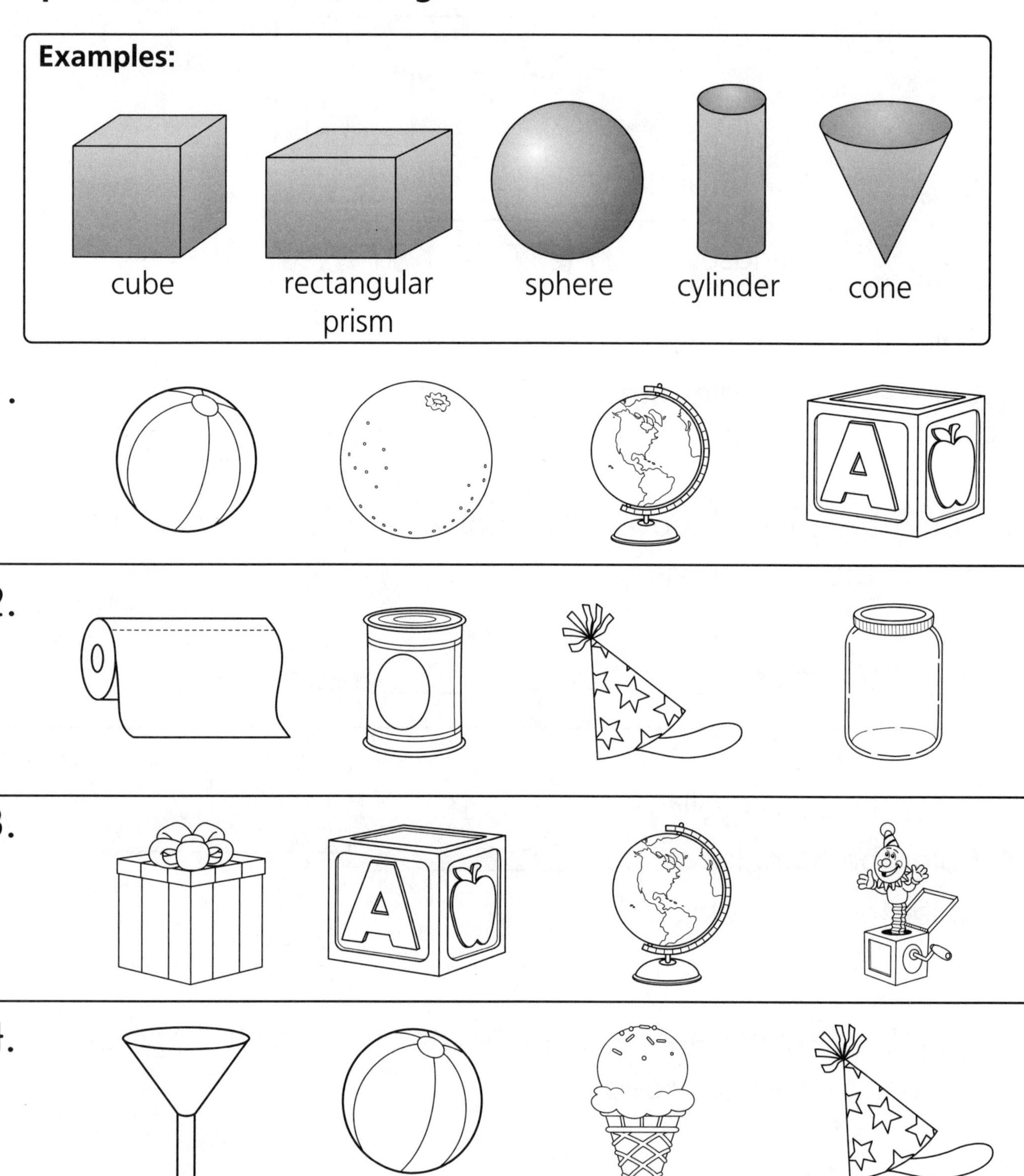

Total Problems: Total Correct: Score:

Name ______________________________

Study the pictograph below and answer the questions on the lines provided.

Baseballs Owned by Five Friends

Friends	Number of Baseballs
Scott	⚾ ⚾ ⚾
Lindsey	⚾ ⚾ ⚾ ⚾ ⚾
Joe	⚾ ⚾ ⚾ ⚾
Sarah	⚾ ⚾ ⚾
Tim	⚾

1. How many baseballs does Tim have? ______________________

2. How many baseballs does Joe have? ______________________

3. How many baseballs do Scott and Sarah have in all?

   ________ + ________ = ________

4. How many baseballs do Tim, Joe, and Lindsey have in all?

   ________ + ________ + ________ = ________

5. How many more baseballs does Lindsey have than Joe?

   ________ − ________ = ________

Total Problems: Total Correct: Score:

Name ______________________________

Study the pictograph below and answer the questions on the lines provided.

Cookies Sold by Ms. Ryall's First-Grade Class

Students	Boxes of Cookies
Mary	
Cory	
Lisa	
Jill	
Lily	

Key: = 1 box of cookies

1. How many boxes of cookies did Jill sell? ____________________

2. How many boxes of cookies did Mary sell? ____________________

3. Who sold the most boxes of cookies? ____________________

4. Who sold the fewest boxes of cookies? ____________________

5. How many more boxes did Lily sell than Cory?

________ – ________ = ________

Total Problems: Total Correct: Score:

Name ______________________________

Study the bar graph and answer the questions on the lines provided.

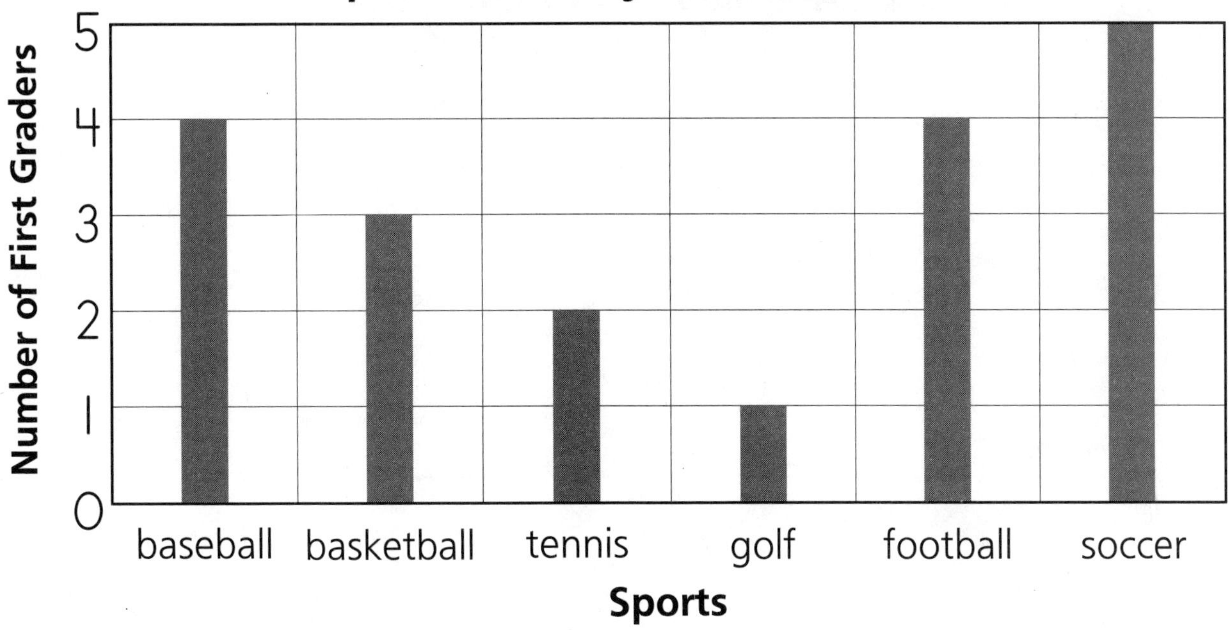

1. How many first graders like golf? ______________________________

2. How many first graders like baseball? ______________________________

3. How many first graders like baseball and tennis?

   ________ + ________ = ________

4. Which sport do first graders like the least?

   ____

5. How many more first graders like soccer than tennis?

   ________ – ________ = ________

Total Problems:	Total Correct:	Score:

Name ______________________________

Study the pie chart and answer the questions on the lines provided.

Animals in the Zoo

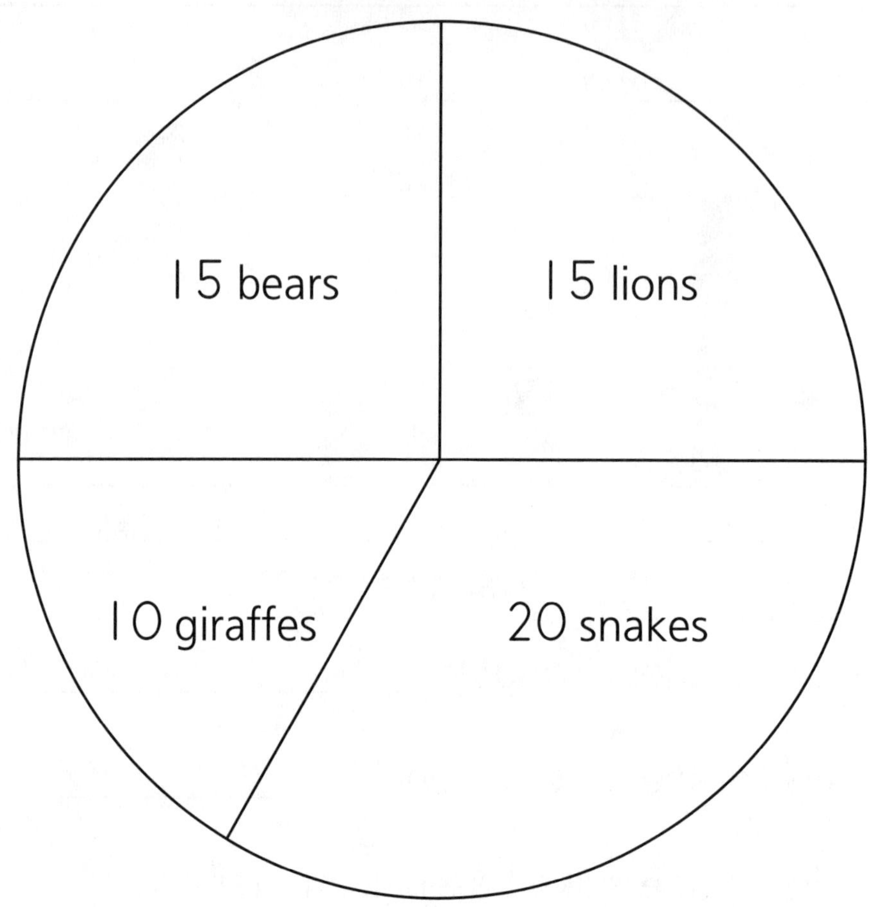

1. How many bears are in the zoo? ______________________________

2. How many lions are in the zoo? ______________________________

3. How many snakes are in the zoo? ______________________________

4. The zoo has 15 of which animal(s)? ______________________________

5. The zoo has the most of which animal? ______________________________

Total Problems: Total Correct: Score:

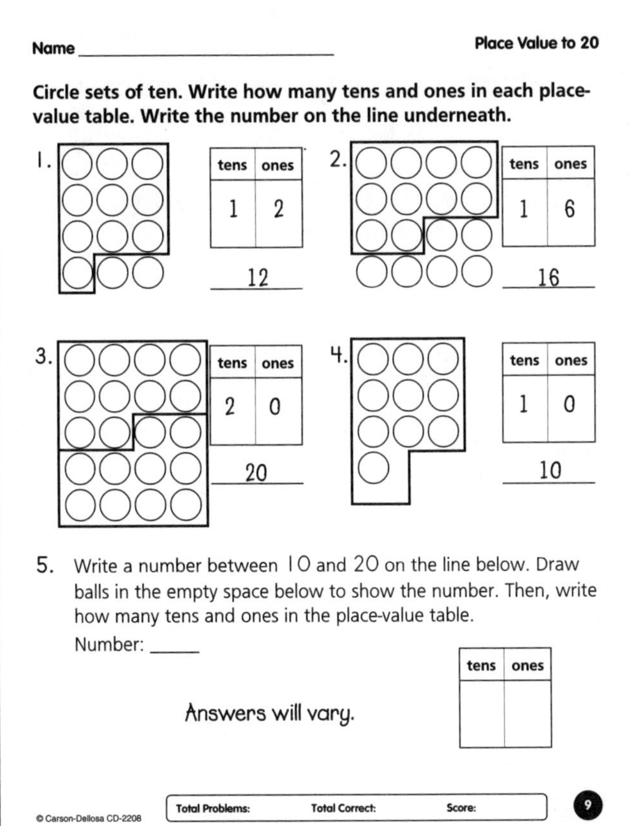

Name ______________________ Place Value to 20

Circle sets of ten. Write how many tens and ones in each place-value table. Write the number on the line underneath.

1.

tens	ones
1	2

12

2.

tens	ones
1	6

16

3.

tens	ones
2	0

20

4.

tens	ones
1	0

10

5. Write a number between 10 and 20 on the line below. Draw balls in the empty space below to show the number. Then, write how many tens and ones in the place-value table.

Number: _____

tens	ones

Answers will vary.

© Carson-Dellosa CD-2208 Total Problems: Total Correct: Score: 9

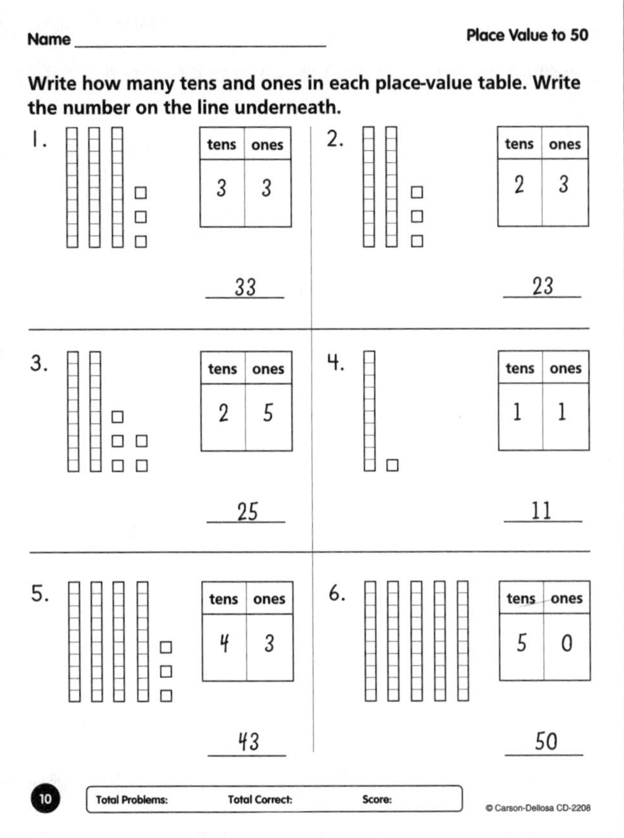

Name ______________________ Place Value to 50

Write how many tens and ones in each place-value table. Write the number on the line underneath.

1.

tens	ones
3	3

33

2.

tens	ones
2	3

23

3.

tens	ones
2	5

25

4.

tens	ones
1	1

11

5.

tens	ones
4	3

43

6.

tens	ones
5	0

50

10 Total Problems: Total Correct: Score: © Carson-Dellosa CD-2208

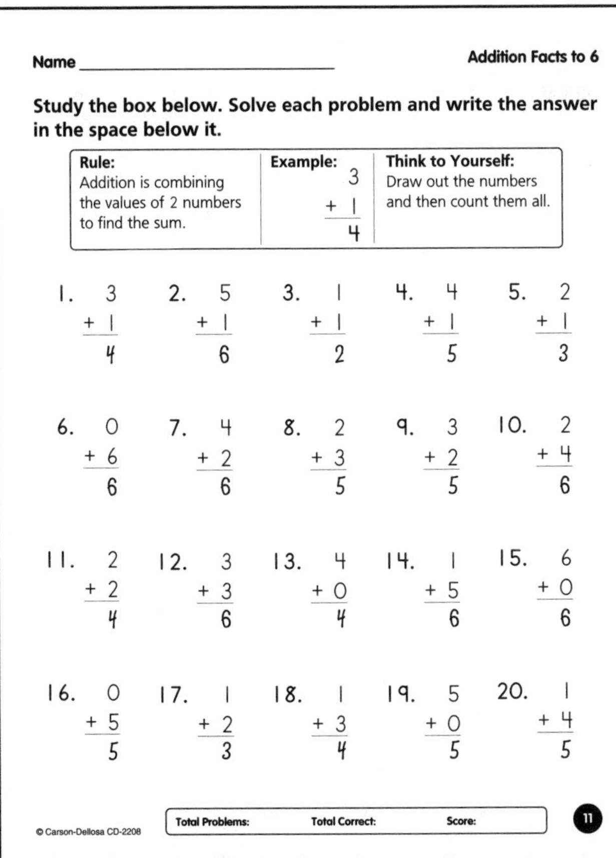

Name ______________________ Addition Facts to 6

Study the box below. Solve each problem and write the answer in the space below it.

Rule:	Example:	Think to Yourself:
Addition is combining the values of 2 numbers to find the sum.	3 + 1 = 4	Draw out the numbers and then count them all.

1. 3 + 1 = 4
2. 5 + 1 = 6
3. 1 + 1 = 2
4. 4 + 1 = 5
5. 2 + 1 = 3
6. 0 + 6 = 6
7. 4 + 2 = 6
8. 2 + 3 = 5
9. 3 + 2 = 5
10. 2 + 4 = 6
11. 2 + 2 = 4
12. 3 + 3 = 6
13. 4 + 0 = 4
14. 1 + 5 = 6
15. 6 + 0 = 6
16. 0 + 5 = 5
17. 1 + 2 = 3
18. 1 + 3 = 4
19. 5 + 0 = 5
20. 1 + 4 = 5

© Carson-Dellosa CD-2208 Total Problems: Total Correct: Score: 11

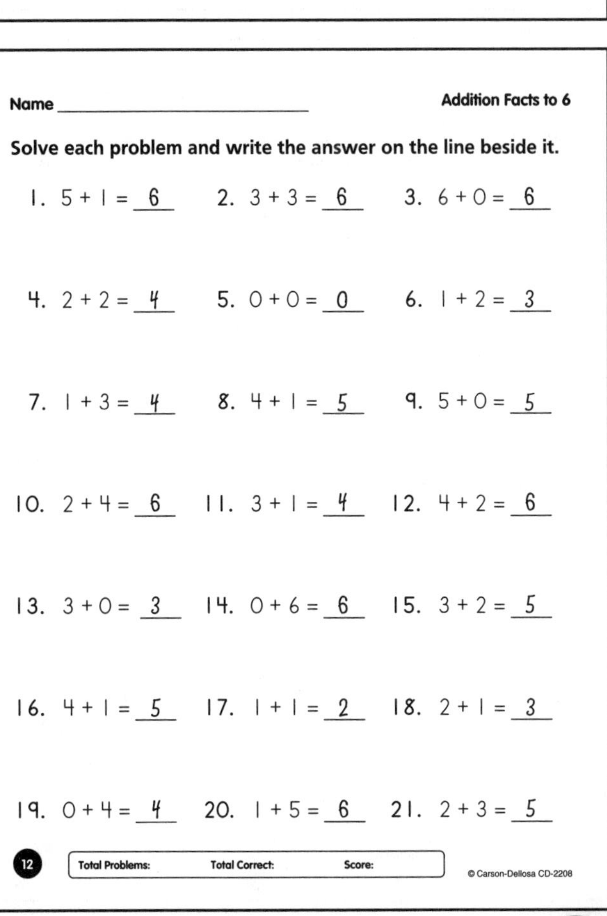

Name ______________________ Addition Facts to 6

Solve each problem and write the answer on the line beside it.

1. 5 + 1 = 6
2. 3 + 3 = 6
3. 6 + 0 = 6
4. 2 + 2 = 4
5. 0 + 0 = 0
6. 1 + 2 = 3
7. 1 + 3 = 4
8. 4 + 1 = 5
9. 5 + 0 = 5
10. 2 + 4 = 6
11. 3 + 1 = 4
12. 4 + 2 = 6
13. 3 + 0 = 3
14. 0 + 6 = 6
15. 3 + 2 = 5
16. 4 + 1 = 5
17. 1 + 1 = 2
18. 2 + 1 = 3
19. 0 + 4 = 4
20. 1 + 5 = 6
21. 2 + 3 = 5

12 Total Problems: Total Correct: Score: © Carson-Dellosa CD-2208

Name ____________ **Addition Facts to 10**

Solve each problem and write the answer in the space below it.

1. 5 + 3 = 8	2. 7 + 1 = 8	3. 8 + 0 = 8	4. 5 + 1 = 6	5. 2 + 5 = 7
6. 2 + 6 = 8	7. 5 + 5 = 10	8. 6 + 2 = 8	9. 3 + 6 = 9	10. 4 + 4 = 8
11. 3 + 3 = 6	12. 1 + 1 = 2	13. 4 + 3 = 7	14. 5 + 4 = 9	15. 2 + 2 = 4
16. 5 + 0 = 5	17. 3 + 5 = 8	18. 3 + 7 = 10	19. 2 + 3 = 5	20. 6 + 4 = 10
21. 7 + 2 = 9	22. 9 + 1 = 10	23. 1 + 7 = 8	24. 0 + 6 = 6	25. 8 + 2 = 10

Total Problems: Total Correct: Score:

Name ____________ **Addition Facts to 10**

Solve each problem and write the answer on the line beside it.

1. 2 + 6 = 8	2. 3 + 5 = 8	3. 5 + 5 = 10
4. 6 + 3 = 9	5. 0 + 1 = 1	6. 2 + 1 = 3
7. 10 + 0 = 10	8. 3 + 6 = 9	9. 4 + 5 = 9
10. 4 + 6 = 10	11. 9 + 0 = 9	12. 5 + 2 = 7
13. 4 + 1 = 5	14. 7 + 2 = 9	15. 8 + 2 = 10
16. 1 + 6 = 7	17. 1 + 3 = 4	18. 0 + 8 = 8
19. 6 + 2 = 8	20. 0 + 9 = 9	21. 4 + 3 = 7
22. 3 + 7 = 10	23. 0 + 4 = 4	24. 8 + 1 = 9
25. 4 + 4 = 8	26. 7 + 1 = 8	27. 7 + 0 = 7

Total Problems: Total Correct: Score:

Name ____________ **Order in Adding**

Study the box below. Find each sum and write the answer on the line beside it. Then, change the order and write a new number sentence.

Rule:	Example:
When you add, the order of the numbers does not change the answer.	2 + 1 = 3 1 + 2 = 3

1. 1 + 3 = 4 — 3 + 1 = 4
2. 4 + 6 = 10 — 6 + 4 = 10
3. 7 + 3 = 10 — 3 + 7 = 10
4. 2 + 3 = 5 — 3 + 2 = 5
5. 9 + 1 = 10 — 1 + 9 = 10
6. 8 + 0 = 8 — 0 + 8 = 8
7. 2 + 3 = 5 — 3 + 2 = 5

Total Problems: Total Correct: Score:

Name ____________ **Number Lines**

Study the example below. Use the number line to add. Circle the greater number. Draw  **to count on. Write the answer on the line beside it.**

Example:

5 + 3 = 8

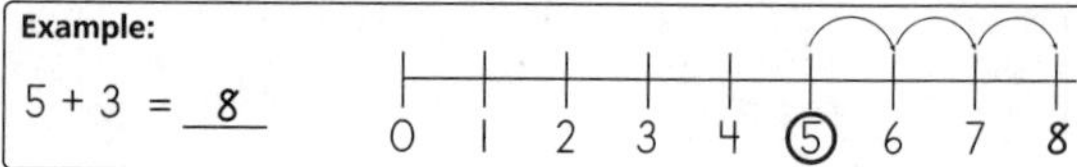

1. 2 + 4 = 6

2. 6 + 2 = 8

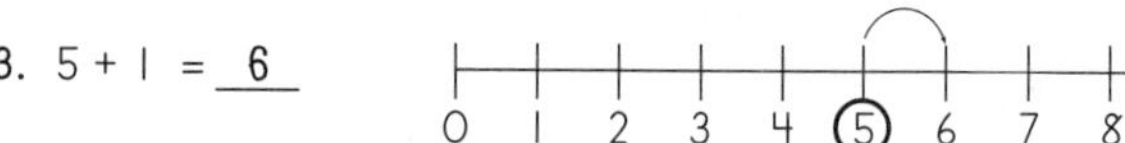

3. 5 + 1 = 6

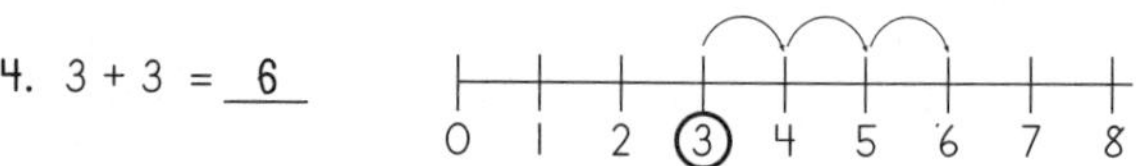

4. 3 + 3 = 6

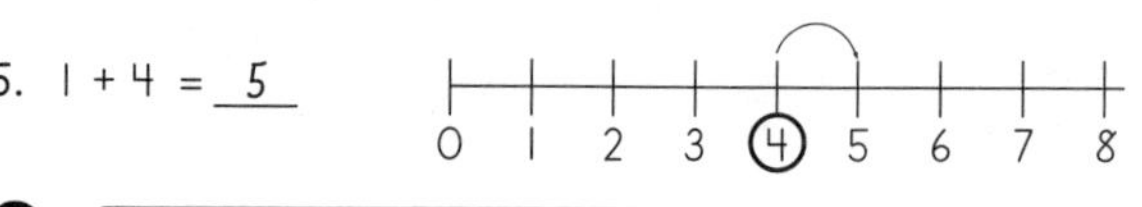

5. 1 + 4 = 5

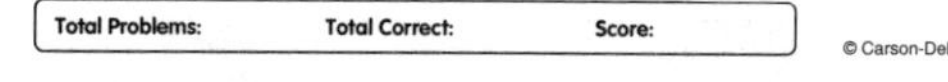

Total Problems: Total Correct: Score:

Name ____________ **Counting On**

Study the example below. Solve each problem. Write the answer on the line beside it.

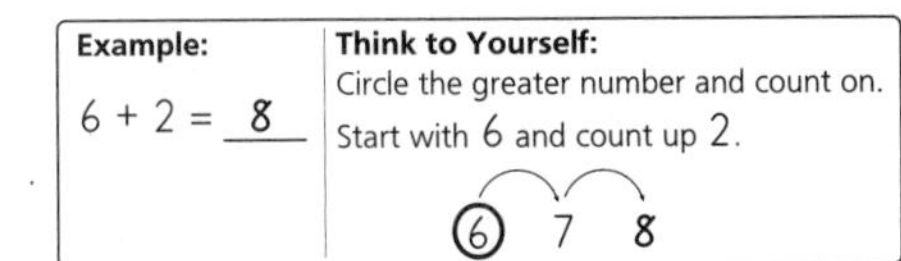

1. 5 + 2 = 7 2. 8 + 2 = 10 3. 10 + 0 = 10

4. 7 + 2 = 9 5. 4 + 6 = 10 6. 4 + 4 = 8

7. 2 + 5 = 7 8. 6 + 3 = 9 9. 9 + 1 = 10

10. 7 + 3 = 10 11. 3 + 5 = 8 12. 3 + 4 = 7

13. 5 + 1 = 6 14. 5 + 2 = 7 15. 4 + 5 = 9

© Carson-Dellosa CD-2208 | Total Problems: | Total Correct: | Score: | 17

Name ____________ **Doubles**

Study the example below. Draw one or more ● to make doubles. Write each number sentence on the lines below it.

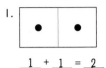

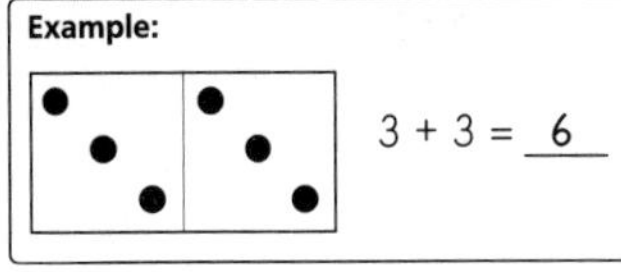

1. 1 + 1 = 2
2. 2 + 2 = 4
3. 5 + 5 = 10
4. 4 + 4 = 8

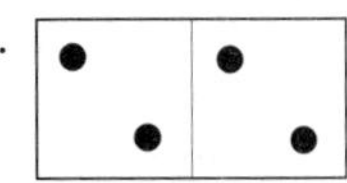

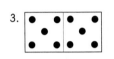

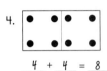

Draw your own ● in the boxes. Write each number sentence on the lines below it.

5. Answers will vary. ___ + ___ = ___
6. Answers will vary. ___ + ___ = ___

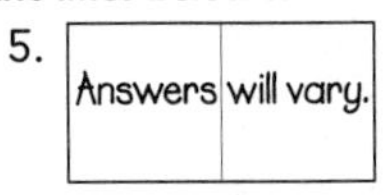

18 | Total Problems: | Total Correct: | Score: | © Carson-Dellosa CD-2208

Name ____________ **Addition Facts to 15**

Solve each problem and write the answer in the space below it.

1. 7 + 8 = 15 2. 9 + 5 = 14 3. 8 + 5 = 13 4. 5 + 7 = 12 5. 2 + 9 = 11

6. 7 + 3 = 10 7. 6 + 9 = 15 8. 9 + 1 = 10 9. 8 + 6 = 14 10. 4 + 9 = 13

11. 4 + 8 = 12 12. 7 + 7 = 14 13. 3 + 8 = 11 14. 6 + 5 = 11 15. 6 + 4 = 10

16. 5 + 4 = 9 17. 1 + 9 = 10 18. 6 + 6 = 12 19. 4 + 4 = 8 20. 3 + 7 = 10

21. 7 + 6 = 13 22. 5 + 9 = 14 23. 6 + 3 = 9 24. 9 + 6 = 15 25. 5 + 6 = 11

© Carson-Dellosa CD-2208 | Total Problems: | Total Correct: | Score: | 19

Name ____________ **Addition Facts to 20**

Solve each problem and write the answer in the space below it.

1. 7 + 9 = 16 2. 6 + 6 = 12 3. 5 + 8 = 13 4. 9 + 7 = 16 5. 9 + 9 = 18

6. 8 + 6 = 14 7. 8 + 7 = 15 8. 8 + 9 = 17 9. 10 + 9 = 19 10. 7 + 8 = 15

11. 5 + 5 = 10 12. 8 + 5 = 13 13. 10 + 4 = 14 14. 9 + 5 = 14 15. 8 + 4 = 12

16. 9 + 1 = 10 17. 3 + 9 = 12 18. 6 + 9 = 15 19. 7 + 6 = 13 20. 5 + 9 = 14

21. 9 + 8 = 17 22. 7 + 7 = 14 23. 7 + 5 = 12 24. 6 + 7 = 13 25. 3 + 8 = 11

20 | Total Problems: | Total Correct: | Score: | © Carson-Dellosa CD-2208

Name ____________________ **Addition Facts to 20**

Solve each problem and write the answer on the line beside it.

1. 7 + 6 = 13	2. 8 + 1 = 9	3. 3 + 5 = 8
4. 9 + 9 = 18	5. 6 + 3 = 9	6. 7 + 4 = 11
7. 10 + 9 = 19	8. 10 + 10 = 20	9. 5 + 5 = 10
10. 8 + 6 = 14	11. 6 + 9 = 15	12. 9 + 8 = 17
13. 2 + 7 = 9	14. 8 + 8 = 16	15. 7 + 8 = 15
16. 8 + 4 = 12	17. 9 + 6 = 15	18. 7 + 3 = 10
19. 8 + 7 = 15	20. 6 + 8 = 14	21. 4 + 9 = 13
22. 6 + 5 = 11	23. 9 + 7 = 16	24. 2 + 8 = 10
25. 4 + 9 = 13	26. 8 + 5 = 13	27. 10 + 8 = 18

Total Problems: Total Correct: Score:

Name ____________________ **Addition with Three Addends**

Solve each problem and write the answer in the space below it.

1. 8 9 + 1 18	2. 6 5 + 2 13	3. 8 8 + 2 18	4. 6 6 + 4 16	5. 4 8 + 1 13
6. 3 6 + 2 11	7. 7 8 + 3 18	8. 2 2 + 8 12	9. 7 4 + 2 13	10. 1 6 + 5 12
11. 4 4 + 5 13	12. 9 8 + 1 18	13. 8 4 + 4 16	14. 5 5 + 5 15	15. 3 3 + 5 11
16. 4 7 + 2 13	17. 1 2 + 4 7	18. 6 1 + 9 16	19. 7 2 + 6 15	20. 5 3 + 9 17

Total Problems: Total Correct: Score:

Name ____________________ **Addition with Three Addends**

Solve each problem and write the answer in the space below it.

1. 8 7 + 2 17	2. 5 4 + 1 10	3. 7 7 + 1 15	4. 5 5 + 3 13	5. 3 7 + 0 10
6. 2 5 + 1 8	7. 6 7 + 2 15	8. 1 1 + 7 9	9. 6 3 + 1 10	10. 0 5 + 1 6
11. 3 3 + 4 10	12. 8 7 + 2 17	13. 7 3 + 4 14	14. 4 4 + 4 12	15. 3 2 + 4 9
16. 3 6 + 4 13	17. 5 3 + 6 14	18. 5 2 + 8 15	19. 6 1 + 5 12	20. 4 2 + 8 14

Total Problems: Total Correct: Score:

Name ____________________ **Addition with Three Addends**

Solve each problem and write the answer in the space below it.

1. 9 8 + 3 20	2. 7 6 + 3 16	3. 9 9 + 3 22	4. 7 7 + 5 19	5. 5 9 + 2 16
6. 4 7 + 3 14	7. 8 2 + 4 14	8. 3 3 + 9 15	9. 8 3 + 1 12	10. 2 7 + 6 15
11. 6 5 + 6 17	12. 8 9 + 4 21	13. 9 5 + 5 19	14. 6 7 + 7 20	15. 4 4 + 6 14
16. 5 8 + 3 16	17. 2 3 + 5 10	18. 7 2 + 8 17	19. 8 3 + 7 18	20. 6 4 + 7 17

Total Problems: Total Correct: Score:

Name ______________________ **Missing Numbers**

Study the example below. Then, solve each problem and write the missing number in the box.

Example: 7 + [7] = 14

Think to Yourself: 7 plus what number equals 14?

1. 9 + [8] = 17
2. 3 + [7] = 10
3. 8 + [6] = 14
4. 6 + [6] = 12
5. 5 + [5] = 10
6. 4 + [9] = 13
7. 3 + [8] = 11
8. 6 + [7] = 13
9. 9 + [5] = 14
10. 8 + [8] = 16
11. 7 + [5] = 12
12. 8 + [5] = 13
13. 3 + [9] = 12
14. 5 + [9] = 14
15. 7 + [4] = 11
16. 5 + [4] = 9
17. 6 + [7] = 13
18. 9 + [9] = 18
19. 4 + [7] = 11
20. 8 + [9] = 17

Total Problems: Total Correct: Score:

Name ______________________ **Two-Digit Addition without Regrouping**

Study the box below. Solve each problem and write the answer in the space below it.

Rule: Draw a line between the tens and the ones places. Add the ones first, then add the tens.

Example: 1|5 + 2|0 = 3|5

1. 3|0 + 2|5 = 5|5
2. 1|6 + 1|3 = 2|9
3. 2|4 + 1|4 = 3|8
4. 1|2 + 1|4 = 2|6
5. 1|9 + 1|0 = 2|9
6. 5|4 + |2 = 5|6
7. 6|0 + 3|0 = 9|0
8. 1|5 + 1|4 = 2|9
9. 2|2 + 3|3 = 5|5
10. 4|0 + 3|0 = 7|0
11. 3|6 + 2|2 = 5|8
12. 1|5 + 2|1 = 3|6
13. 6|0 + 2|0 = 8|0
14. 1|8 + 1|0 = 2|8
15. 4|0 + 1|7 = 5|7
16. 2|1 + 7|0 = 9|1
17. 3|0 + 2|5 = 5|5
18. 5|6 + 4|1 = 9|7
19. 3|2 + 3|2 = 6|4
20. 5|0 + 2|5 = 7|5

Total Problems: Total Correct: Score:

Name ______________________ **Two-Digit Addition without Regrouping**

Solve each problem and write the answer in the space below it.

1. 23 + 53 = 76
2. 41 + 43 = 84
3. 88 + 10 = 98
4. 77 + 12 = 89
5. 17 + 22 = 39
6. 14 + 64 = 78
7. 12 + 12 = 24
8. 82 + 13 = 95
9. 47 + 31 = 78
10. 68 + 10 = 78
11. 55 + 10 = 65
12. 82 + 14 = 96
13. 62 + 24 = 86
14. 80 + 10 = 90
15. 40 + 23 = 63
16. 50 + 31 = 81
17. 73 + 11 = 84
18. 25 + 12 = 37
19. 15 + 14 = 29
20. 25 + 33 = 58
21. 72 + 20 = 92
22. 52 + 40 = 92
23. 67 + 21 = 88
24. 23 + 11 = 34
25. 40 + 15 = 55

Total Problems: Total Correct: Score:

Name ______________________ **Three-Digit Addition without Regrouping**

Solve each problem and write the answer in the space below it.

1. 231 + 222 = 453
2. 190 + 200 = 390
3. 362 + 322 = 684
4. 130 + 160 = 290
5. 300 + 200 = 500
6. 445 + 223 = 668
7. 110 + 320 = 430
8. 600 + 300 = 900
9. 303 + 404 = 707
10. 222 + 222 = 444
11. 661 + 331 = 992
12. 710 + 250 = 960
13. 437 + 562 = 999
14. 350 + 200 = 550
15. 500 + 250 = 750
16. 162 + 201 = 363
17. 656 + 333 = 989
18. 536 + 232 = 768
19. 432 + 234 = 666
20. 123 + 456 = 579
21. 710 + 213 = 923
22. 242 + 314 = 556
23. 534 + 225 = 759
24. 472 + 222 = 694

Total Problems: Total Correct: Score:

Name ____________________ **Three-Digit Addition without Regrouping**

Solve each problem and write the answer in the space below it.

1. 630 + 240 = 870	2. 400 + 200 = 600	3. 800 + 100 = 900	4. 505 + 252 = 757
5. 741 + 147 = 888	6. 460 + 222 = 682	7. 725 + 250 = 975	8. 450 + 333 = 783
9. 188 + 200 = 388	10. 124 + 421 = 545	11. 461 + 120 = 581	12. 720 + 160 = 880
13. 250 + 235 = 485	14. 426 + 123 = 549	15. 836 + 121 = 957	16. 625 + 124 = 749
17. 816 + 142 = 958	18. 670 + 200 = 870	19. 231 + 231 = 462	20. 446 + 222 = 668
21. 809 + 100 = 909	22. 752 + 231 = 983	23. 690 + 209 = 899	24. 489 + 510 = 999

Total Problems: Total Correct: Score:

Name ____________________ **Problem Solving with Addition**

Add to each picture to help solve the problem. Write the number sentence below.

1. Sally picks 2 flowers. Then, she picks 2 more. How many flowers does she have in all?

2 + 2 = 4

Pictures will vary but should include two flowers.

2. Scott picks 6 apples. Then, he picks 1 more. How many apples does he have in all?

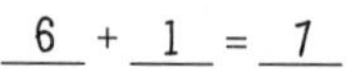

6 + 1 = 7

Pictures will vary but should include one apple.

3. Joe sees 2 fish bowls. There are 3 fish in each bowl. How many fish are there?

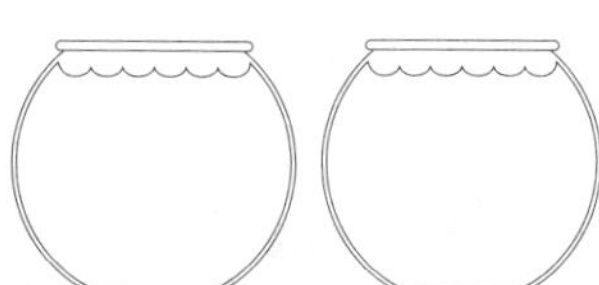

3 + 3 = 6

Pictures will vary but should include three fish in each fish bowl.

Total Problems: Total Correct: Score:

Name ____________________ **Subtraction Facts to 6**

Study the box below. Solve each problem and write the answer in the space below it.

Rule:	Example:	Think to Yourself:
Subtraction is taking away the value of one number from another number to find the difference.	4 − 1 = 3	Draw out the greater number and then take away the lesser number.

1. 6 − 1 = 5	2. 4 − 2 = 2	3. 3 − 1 = 2	4. 5 − 0 = 5	5. 5 − 2 = 3
6. 6 − 6 = 0	7. 4 − 1 = 3	8. 6 − 4 = 2	9. 4 − 3 = 1	10. 3 − 2 = 1
11. 6 − 5 = 1	12. 6 − 3 = 3	13. 1 − 1 = 0	14. 5 − 3 = 2	15. 4 − 0 = 4
16. 5 − 4 = 1	17. 6 − 2 = 4	18. 5 − 1 = 4	19. 5 − 5 = 0	20. 3 − 3 = 0

Total Problems: Total Correct: Score:

Name ____________________ **Subtraction Facts to 6**

Solve each problem and write the answer on the line beside it.

1. 2 − 2 = 0	2. 6 − 1 = 5	3. 4 − 2 = 2
4. 0 − 0 = 0	5. 5 − 4 = 1	6. 6 − 3 = 3
7. 5 − 2 = 3	8. 3 − 2 = 1	9. 6 − 4 = 2
10. 4 − 3 = 1	11. 3 − 0 = 3	12. 5 − 1 = 4
13. 1 − 0 = 1	14. 2 − 1 = 1	15. 3 − 1 = 2
16. 5 − 0 = 5	17. 5 − 2 = 3	18. 6 − 6 = 0
19. 4 − 1 = 3	20. 6 − 0 = 6	21. 5 − 3 = 2
22. 6 − 2 = 4	23. 4 − 0 = 4	24. 6 − 5 = 1

Total Problems: Total Correct: Score:

Name ____________ Subtraction Facts to 10

Solve each problem and write the answer in the space below it.

1. 10 − 2 = 8	2. 8 − 5 = 3	3. 9 − 6 = 3	4. 7 − 6 = 1	5. 7 − 7 = 0
6. 8 − 6 = 2	7. 7 − 3 = 4	8. 8 − 4 = 4	9. 9 − 9 = 0	10. 9 − 2 = 7
11. 7 − 5 = 2	12. 6 − 5 = 1	13. 8 − 3 = 5	14. 9 − 4 = 5	15. 10 − 8 = 2
16. 4 − 4 = 0	17. 8 − 7 = 1	18. 9 − 5 = 4	19. 8 − 2 = 6	20. 10 − 10 = 0
21. 5 − 4 = 1	22. 6 − 2 = 4	23. 10 − 3 = 7	24. 9 − 3 = 6	25. 10 − 5 = 5

Total Problems: Total Correct: Score:

Name ____________ Subtraction Facts to 10

Solve each problem and write the answer on the line beside it.

1. 9 − 5 = 4	2. 3 − 3 = 0	3. 8 − 5 = 3
4. 7 − 5 = 2	5. 8 − 6 = 2	6. 8 − 4 = 4
7. 7 − 3 = 4	8. 10 − 8 = 2	9. 5 − 3 = 2
10. 7 − 4 = 3	11. 6 − 5 = 1	12. 8 − 4 = 4
13. 6 − 2 = 4	14. 8 − 7 = 1	15. 10 − 5 = 5
16. 4 − 2 = 2	17. 8 − 3 = 5	18. 10 − 6 = 4
19. 6 − 3 = 3	20. 10 − 3 = 7	21. 9 − 4 = 5
22. 9 − 1 = 8	23. 10 − 2 = 8	24. 0 − 0 = 0
25. 8 − 8 = 0	26. 10 − 9 = 1	27. 6 − 4 = 2

Total Problems: Total Correct: Score:

Name ____________ Number Lines

Study the box below. Use the number line to subtract. Circle the greater number. Draw  to count back. Then, write the answer on the line provided.

Example:
8 − 5 = 3
0 1 2 3 4 5 6 7 (8) 9 10

1. 10 − 6 = 4
0 1 2 3 4 5 6 7 8 9 (10)

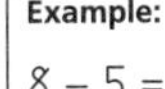

2. 8 − 2 = 6
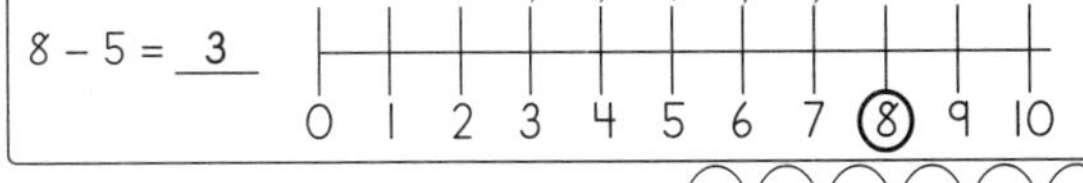
0 1 2 3 4 5 6 7 (8) 9 10

3. 10 − 8 = 2
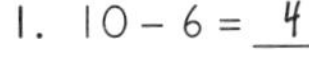

0 1 2 3 4 5 6 7 8 9 (10)

4. 7 − 2 = 5
0 1 2 3 4 5 6 (7) 8 9 10

5. 9 − 6 = 3
0 1 2 3 4 5 6 7 8 (9) 10

Total Problems: Total Correct: Score:

Name ____________ Counting Back

Study the box below. Solve each problem and write the answer in the space below it .

Rule:	Example:	Think to Yourself:
When subtracting, start with the greater number and count back to the lesser number to find the answer.	10 − 7 = 3	Start with 10. Count back to 7. 7 8 9 (10)

1. 8 − 7 = 1	2. 10 − 8 = 2	3. 9 − 2 = 7	4. 6 − 5 = 1	5. 10 − 7 = 3
6. 8 − 5 = 3	7. 10 − 3 = 7	8. 9 − 4 = 5	9. 7 − 4 = 3	10. 8 − 2 = 6
11. 9 − 7 = 2	12. 6 − 3 = 3	13. 8 − 3 = 5	14. 9 − 5 = 4	15. 8 − 4 = 4
16. 7 − 3 = 4	17. 9 − 1 = 8	18. 6 − 2 = 4	19. 8 − 6 = 2	20. 5 − 1 = 4

Total Problems: Total Correct: Score:

Name ______________________ **Subtraction Facts to 15**

Solve each problem and write the answer in the space below it.

1. 13 − 6 = 7	2. 11 − 5 = 6	3. 13 − 4 = 9	4. 12 − 6 = 6	5. 14 − 9 = 5
6. 14 − 8 = 6	7. 15 − 9 = 6	8. 10 − 8 = 2	9. 12 − 5 = 7	10. 15 − 6 = 9
11. 13 − 8 = 5	12. 11 − 8 = 3	13. 13 − 5 = 8	14. 13 − 9 = 4	15. 15 − 7 = 8
16. 11 − 7 = 4	17. 8 − 4 = 4	18. 13 − 7 = 6	19. 12 − 7 = 5	20. 15 − 3 = 12
21. 14 − 5 = 9	22. 12 − 9 = 3	23. 15 − 5 = 10	24. 12 − 8 = 4	25. 13 − 2 = 11

Total Problems: Total Correct: Score:

Name ______________________ **Subtraction Facts to 20**

Solve each problem and write the answer in the space below it.

1. 17 − 8 = 9	2. 12 − 5 = 7	3. 15 − 8 = 7	4. 20 − 9 = 11	5. 10 − 5 = 5
6. 13 − 7 = 6	7. 11 − 9 = 2	8. 13 − 9 = 4	9. 14 − 5 = 9	10. 17 − 9 = 8
11. 10 − 2 = 8	12. 18 − 9 = 9	13. 16 − 9 = 7	14. 8 − 4 = 4	15. 18 − 7 = 11
16. 15 − 7 = 8	17. 14 − 8 = 6	18. 17 − 8 = 9	19. 12 − 8 = 4	20. 15 − 9 = 6
21. 19 − 8 = 11	22. 15 − 6 = 9	23. 17 − 9 = 8	24. 13 − 7 = 6	25. 15 − 5 = 10

Total Problems: Total Correct: Score:

Name ______________________ **Subtraction Facts to 20**

Solve each problem and write the answer on the line beside it.

1. 14 − 5 = 9	2. 16 − 9 = 7	3. 20 − 10 = 10
4. 18 − 9 = 9	5. 15 − 7 = 8	6. 13 − 7 = 6
7. 13 − 8 = 5	8. 16 − 9 = 7	9. 18 − 9 = 9
10. 12 − 5 = 7	11. 11 − 9 = 2	12. 14 − 9 = 5
13. 14 − 8 = 6	14. 12 − 9 = 3	15. 15 − 8 = 7
16. 17 − 8 = 9	17. 14 − 5 = 9	18. 10 − 4 = 6
19. 15 − 9 = 6	20. 16 − 7 = 9	21. 16 − 8 = 8
22. 13 − 6 = 7	23. 15 − 6 = 9	24. 17 − 8 = 9
25. 14 − 7 = 7	26. 16 − 6 = 10	27. 14 − 6 = 8

Total Problems: Total Correct: Score:

Name ______________________ **Missing Numbers**

Study the example below. Then, solve each problem and write the missing number in the box.

Example: 10 − [7] = 3

Think to Yourself: 10 take away 3 equals what number?

1. 18 − [9] = 9	2. 15 − [8] = 7	3. 10 − [6] = 4	4. 13 − [4] = 9	5. 8 − [7] = 1
6. 12 − [3] = 9	7. 16 − [8] = 8	8. 13 − [9] = 4	9. 14 − [4] = 10	10. 16 − [3] = 13
11. 14 − [2] = 12	12. 16 − [5] = 11	13. 8 − [8] = 0	14. 12 − [9] = 3	15. 11 − [5] = 6
16. 14 − [3] = 11	17. 10 − [1] = 9	18. 17 − [9] = 8	19. 19 − [9] = 10	20. 17 − [7] = 10

Total Problems: Total Correct: Score:

Name ____________________

Two-Digit Subtraction without Regrouping

Study the box below. Solve each problem and write the answer in the space below it.

Rule:	**Example:**
Draw a line between the tens and ones places. Subtract the ones first, then subtract the tens.	8|3 − 2|3 6|0

1. 6|9 − 3|0 3|9	2. 7|3 − 2|2 5|1	3. 8|0 − 6|0 2|0	4. 8|3 − 3|0 5|3	5. 2|9 − 2|4 |5
6. 6|5 − 3|4 3|1	7. 9|6 − 9|0 |6	8. 7|8 − 5|2 2|6	9. 2|5 − 2|3 |2	10. 4|7 − 1|7 3|0
11. 5|1 − 5|0 |1	12. 9|9 − 2|8 7|1	13. 6|2 − 1|0 5|2	14. 8|5 − 5|0 3|5	15. 9|6 − 5|0 4|6
16. 6|2 − 2|1 4|1	17. 7|5 − 3|1 4|4	18. 8|3 − 5|2 3|1	19. 8|8 − 1|1 7|7	20. 8|6 − 3|5 5|1

Total Problems: Total Correct: Score:

Name ____________________

Two-Digit Subtraction without Regrouping

Solve each problem and write the answer in the space below it.

1. 64 − 40 24	2. 91 − 60 31	3. 87 − 12 75	4. 35 − 24 11	5. 81 − 21 60
6. 39 − 28 11	7. 48 − 27 21	8. 48 − 23 25	9. 83 − 41 42	10. 70 − 20 50
11. 67 − 40 27	12. 66 − 33 33	13. 71 − 51 20	14. 73 − 30 43	15. 98 − 54 44
16. 68 − 51 17	17. 69 − 23 46	18. 26 − 13 13	19. 49 − 46 3	20. 76 − 63 13
21. 49 − 20 29	22. 35 − 25 10	23. 78 − 62 16	24. 97 − 15 82	25. 54 − 10 44

Total Problems: Total Correct: Score:

Name ____________________

Three-Digit Subtraction without Regrouping

Solve each problem and write the answer in the space below it.

1. 364 − 124 240	2. 445 − 213 232	3. 695 − 434 261	4. 798 − 581 217
5. 345 − 222 123	6. 575 − 250 325	7. 200 − 100 100	8. 213 − 102 111
9. 840 − 230 610	10. 268 − 111 157	11. 745 − 434 311	12. 465 − 120 345
13. 660 − 200 460	14. 164 − 160 4	15. 450 − 150 300	16. 656 − 333 323
17. 555 − 232 323	18. 898 − 354 544	19. 435 − 224 211	20. 369 − 145 224
21. 255 − 144 111	22. 222 − 222 000	23. 437 − 430 7	24. 800 − 500 300

Total Problems: Total Correct: Score:

Name ____________________

Three-Digit Subtraction without Regrouping

Solve each problem and write the answer in the space below it.

1. 658 − 250 408	2. 465 − 335 130	3. 852 − 441 411	4. 555 − 340 215
5. 425 − 120 305	6. 975 − 525 450	7. 645 − 521 124	8. 457 − 321 136
9. 499 − 311 188	10. 636 − 212 424	11. 690 − 540 150	12. 541 − 240 301
13. 473 − 123 350	14. 468 − 357 111	15. 466 − 155 311	16. 322 − 100 222
17. 741 − 140 601	18. 580 − 270 310	19. 900 − 300 600	20. 487 − 250 237
21. 669 − 558 111	22. 482 − 360 122	23. 485 − 150 335	24. 749 − 600 149

44

Total Problems: Total Correct: Score:

Answer Key

Name ____________________ **Problem Solving with Subtraction**

Use counters to find the answer. Write the answer on the line beside it.

1. Sam has 3 balloons. Then, 2 of the balloons popped. How many balloons does he have now?
   3 - 2 = 1

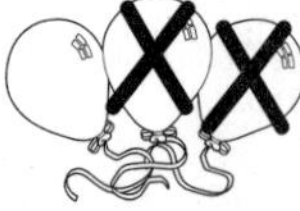

2. There are 10 birds. 5 fly away. How many birds are left?
   10 - 5 = 5

3. Miss Smith bakes 8 muffins. She sells 5. How many muffins does she have left?
   8 - 5 = 3

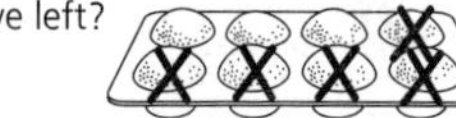

4. Rob has 6 flowers. He gives 4 flowers to Betty. How many flowers does he have left?
   6 - 4 = 2

Name ____________________ **Fact Families**

Study the box below. Add or subtract to find each fact family. Write the answer on the lines beside it.

Rule:	**Example:**
Select two numbers and write their addition number sentences. Use the answer and write the subtraction number sentences using the first two numbers. The group of number sentences is the **fact family**.	2, 3, 5 2 + 3 = 5 5 − 3 = 2 3 + 2 = 5 5 − 2 = 3

1. 3, 4, 7	2. 5, 6, 11	3. 7, 8, 15
4 + 3 = 7	5 + 6 = 11	7 + 8 = 15
3 + 4 = 7	6 + 5 = 11	8 + 7 = 15
7 − 4 = 3	11 − 6 = 5	15 − 8 = 7
7 − 3 = 4	11 − 5 = 6	15 − 7 = 8

4. 10, 11, 21	5. 6, 7, 13	6. 8, 9, 17
10 + 11 = 21	6 + 7 = 13	8 + 9 = 17
11 + 10 = 21	7 + 6 = 13	9 + 8 = 17
21 − 11 = 10	13 − 7 = 6	17 − 9 = 8
21 − 10 = 11	13 − 6 = 7	17 − 8 = 9

Name ____________________ **Two-Digit Mixed Practice without Regrouping**

Add or subtract each problem. Write the answer in the space below it.

1.	2.	3.	4.	5.
88	72	85	54	48
−11	+13	−42	+40	−38
77	85	43	94	10

6.	7.	8.	9.	10.
12	65	87	65	50
+42	−41	+12	−42	+31
54	24	99	23	81

11.	12.	13.	14.	15.
96	23	78	32	74
−23	+63	−35	+57	−52
73	86	43	89	22

16.	17.	18.	19.	20.
73	78	11	64	60
−22	−62	+73	−23	+20
51	16	84	41	80

21.	22.	23.	24.	25.
86	85	85	88	54
−82	−82	+13	−10	+24
4	3	98	78	78

Name ____________________ **Two-Digit Mixed Practice without Regrouping**

Add or subtract each problem. Write the answer in the space below it.

1.	2.	3.	4.	5.
30	63	50	46	73
+25	−41	+38	−23	+26
55	22	88	23	99

6.	7.	8.	9.	10.
54	61	75	20	18
−42	+23	−55	+40	+10
12	84	20	60	28

11.	12.	13.	14.	15.
91	21	82	48	36
−60	+71	−52	−23	+22
31	92	30	25	58

16.	17.	18.	19.	20.
95	80	23	86	45
−30	+19	+23	−21	+20
65	99	46	65	65

21.	22.	23.	24.	25.
76	49	13	54	35
−16	−32	+13	−10	+10
60	17	26	44	45

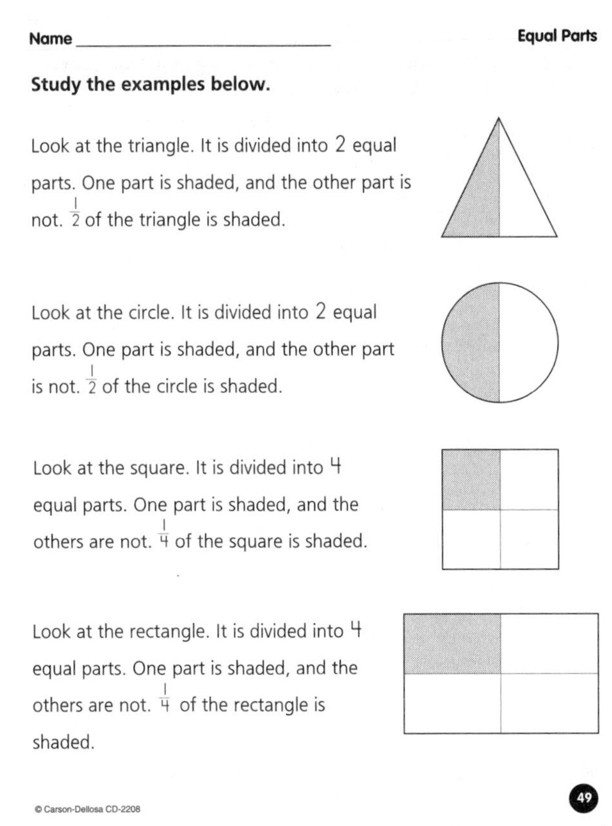

Name ______________________ **Equal Parts**

Study the examples below.

Look at the triangle. It is divided into 2 equal parts. One part is shaded, and the other part is not. $\frac{1}{2}$ of the triangle is shaded.

Look at the circle. It is divided into 2 equal parts. One part is shaded, and the other part is not. $\frac{1}{2}$ of the circle is shaded.

Look at the square. It is divided into 4 equal parts. One part is shaded, and the others are not. $\frac{1}{4}$ of the square is shaded.

Look at the rectangle. It is divided into 4 equal parts. One part is shaded, and the others are not. $\frac{1}{4}$ of the rectangle is shaded.

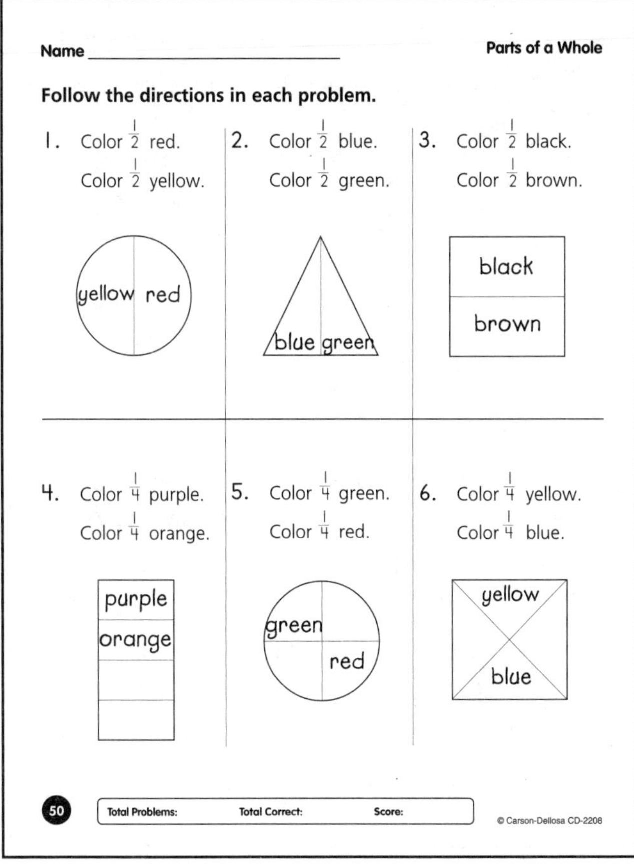

Name ______________________ **Parts of a Whole**

Follow the directions in each problem.

1. Color $\frac{1}{2}$ red. Color $\frac{1}{2}$ yellow.
2. Color $\frac{1}{2}$ blue. Color $\frac{1}{2}$ green.
3. Color $\frac{1}{2}$ black. Color $\frac{1}{2}$ brown.

4. Color $\frac{1}{4}$ purple. Color $\frac{1}{4}$ orange.
5. Color $\frac{1}{4}$ green. Color $\frac{1}{4}$ red.
6. Color $\frac{1}{4}$ yellow. Color $\frac{1}{4}$ blue.

Total Problems: Total Correct: Score:

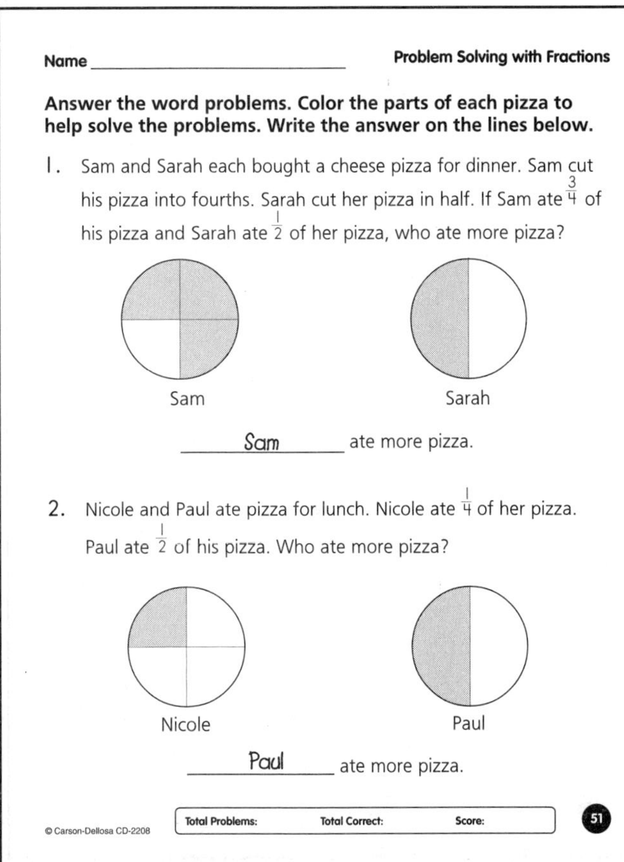

Name ______________________ **Problem Solving with Fractions**

Answer the word problems. Color the parts of each pizza to help solve the problems. Write the answer on the lines below.

1. Sam and Sarah each bought a cheese pizza for dinner. Sam cut his pizza into fourths. Sarah cut her pizza in half. If Sam ate $\frac{3}{4}$ of his pizza and Sarah ate $\frac{1}{2}$ of her pizza, who ate more pizza?

Sam ate more pizza.

2. Nicole and Paul ate pizza for lunch. Nicole ate $\frac{1}{4}$ of her pizza. Paul ate $\frac{1}{2}$ of his pizza. Who ate more pizza?

Paul ate more pizza.

Total Problems: Total Correct: Score:

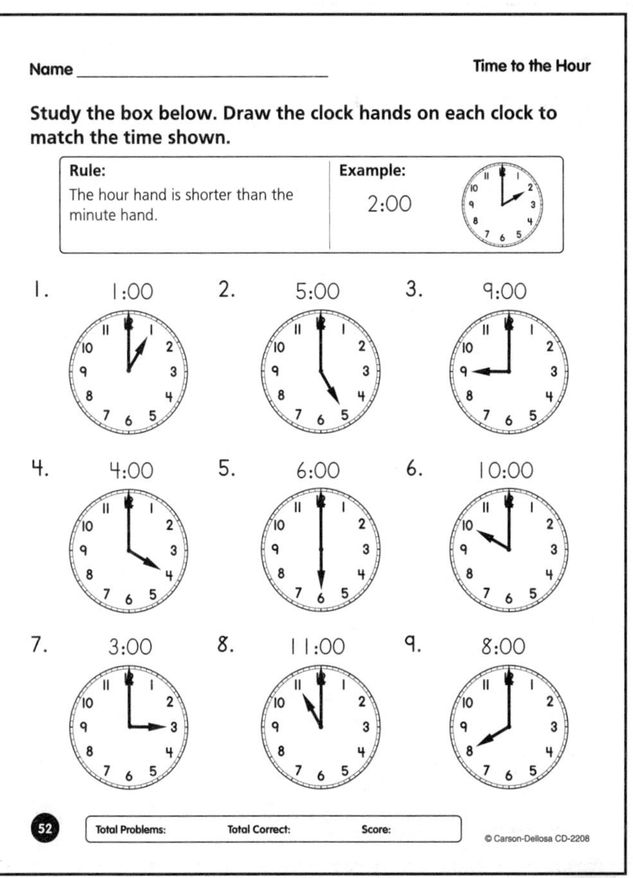

Name ______________________ **Time to the Hour**

Study the box below. Draw the clock hands on each clock to match the time shown.

Rule:	Example:
The hour hand is shorter than the minute hand.	2:00

1. 1:00
2. 5:00
3. 9:00
4. 4:00
5. 6:00
6. 10:00
7. 3:00
8. 11:00
9. 8:00

Total Problems: Total Correct: Score:

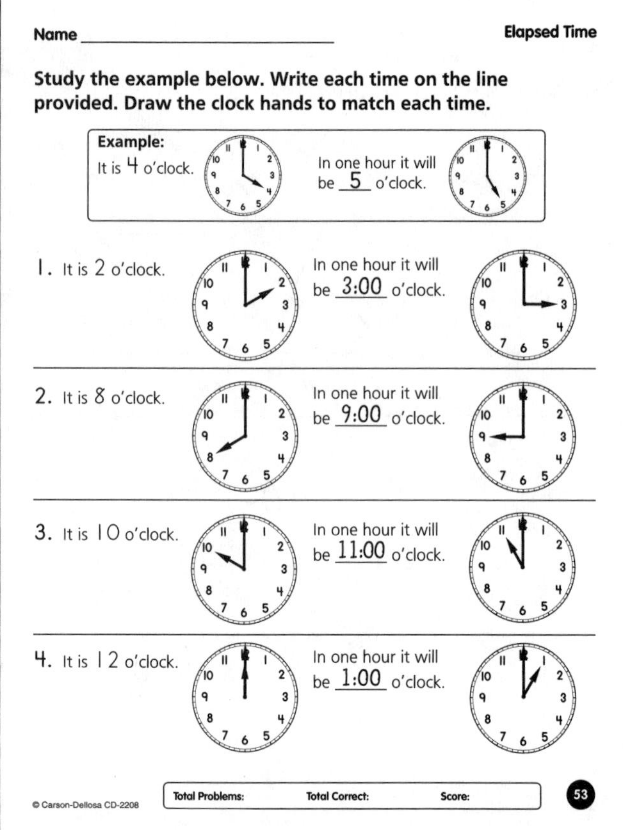

Name ____________________ **Elapsed Time**

Study the example below. Write each time on the line provided. Draw the clock hands to match each time.

Example:
It is 4 o'clock. In one hour it will be 5 o'clock.

1. It is 2 o'clock. In one hour it will be 3:00 o'clock.
2. It is 8 o'clock. In one hour it will be 9:00 o'clock.
3. It is 10 o'clock. In one hour it will be 11:00 o'clock.
4. It is 12 o'clock. In one hour it will be 1:00 o'clock.

© Carson-Dellosa CD-2208 Total Problems: Total Correct: Score: 53

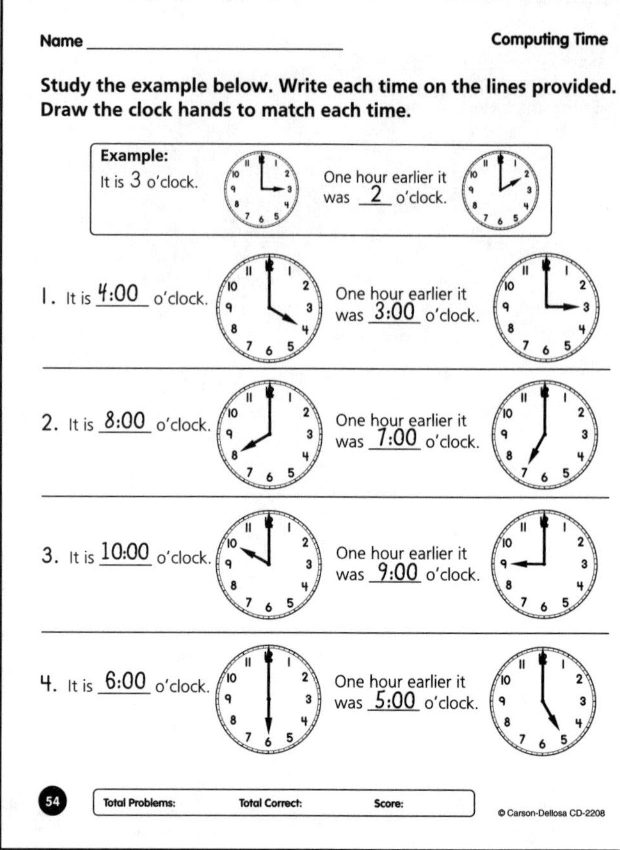

Name ____________________ **Computing Time**

Study the example below. Write each time on the lines provided. Draw the clock hands to match each time.

Example:
It is 3 o'clock. One hour earlier it was 2 o'clock.

1. It is 4:00 o'clock. One hour earlier it was 3:00 o'clock.
2. It is 8:00 o'clock. One hour earlier it was 7:00 o'clock.
3. It is 10:00 o'clock. One hour earlier it was 9:00 o'clock.
4. It is 6:00 o'clock. One hour earlier it was 5:00 o'clock.

54 Total Problems: Total Correct: Score: © Carson-Dellosa CD-2208

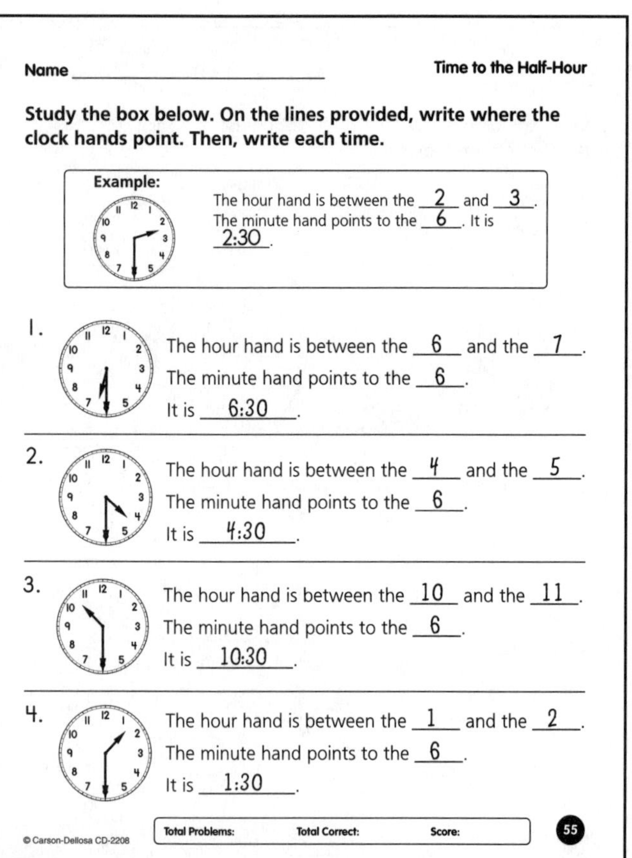

Name ____________________ **Time to the Half-Hour**

Study the box below. On the lines provided, write where the clock hands point. Then, write each time.

Example:
The hour hand is between the 2 and 3.
The minute hand points to the 6. It is 2:30.

1. The hour hand is between the 6 and the 7.
The minute hand points to the 6.
It is 6:30.

2. The hour hand is between the 4 and the 5.
The minute hand points to the 6.
It is 4:30.

3. The hour hand is between the 10 and the 11.
The minute hand points to the 6.
It is 10:30.

4. The hour hand is between the 1 and the 2.
The minute hand points to the 6.
It is 1:30.

© Carson-Dellosa CD-2208 Total Problems: Total Correct: Score: 55

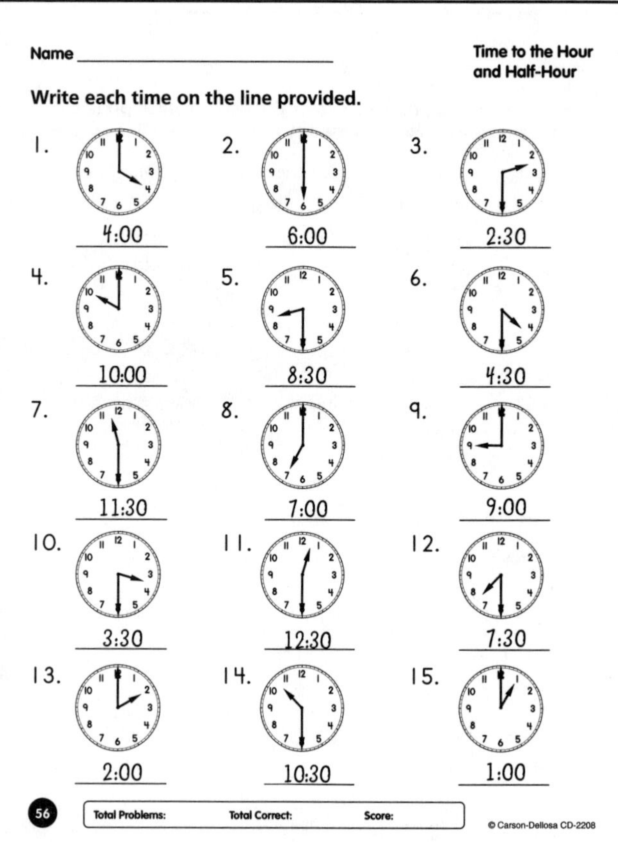

Name ____________________ **Time to the Hour and Half-Hour**

Write each time on the line provided.

1. 4:00
2. 6:00
3. 2:30
4. 10:00
5. 8:30
6. 4:30
7. 11:30
8. 7:00
9. 9:00
10. 3:30
11. 12:30
12. 7:30
13. 2:00
14. 10:30
15. 1:00

56 Total Problems: Total Correct: Score: © Carson-Dellosa CD-2208

Answer Key

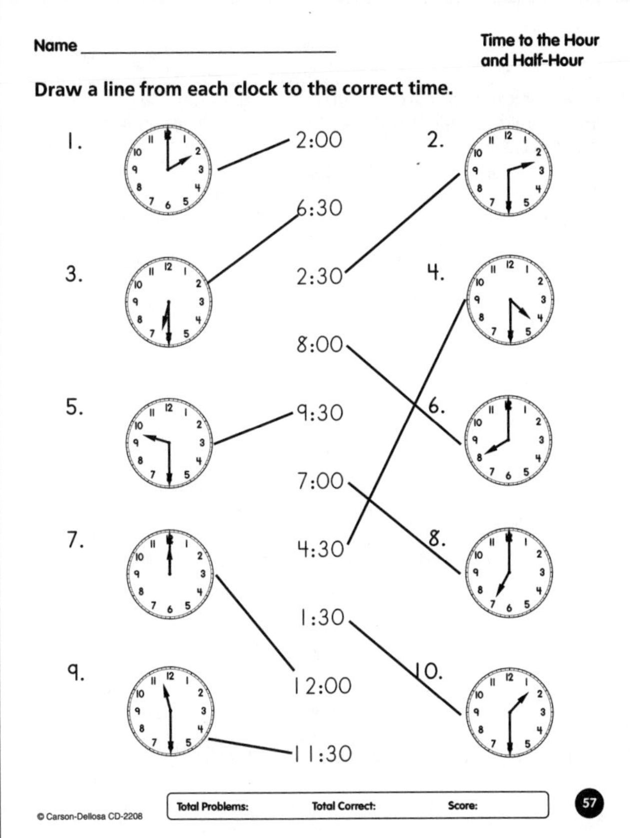

Name ______________________ **Time to the Hour and Half-Hour**

Draw a line from each clock to the correct time.

1. 2. 3. 4. 5. 6. 7. 8. 9. 10.

2:00
6:30
2:30
8:00
9:30
7:00
4:30
1:30
12:00
11:30

© Carson-Dellosa CD-2208 | Total Problems: | Total Correct: | Score: | 57

Name ______________________ **Problem Solving with Time**

Solve each word problem. Draw the hands on the clock. Write each time on the line provided.

1. Sam starts his homework at 3:00. It takes him a half-hour. What time does he finish? 3:30
2. Lisa goes to lunch at 12:00. She eats for 1 hour. What time does Lisa finish lunch? 1:00
3. Kevin walks his dog at 7:00. He walks his dog for a half-hour. What time does he finish walking his dog? 7:30
4. Chris watches his favorite television show at 8:30. It lasts for 1 hour. What time does Chris finish watching this show? 9:30
5. Alex reads his book at 8:00. He reads for 1 hour. What time does he finish? 9:00
6. Kacey washes dishes at 6:30. It takes her a half-hour. What time does she finish? 7:00

58 | Total Problems: | Total Correct: | Score: | © Carson-Dellosa CD-2208

Name ______________________ **Problem Solving with Time**

Solve each word problem. Draw the hands on the clock. Write each time on the line provided.

1. Kate walks to school at 7:30. It takes her a half-hour. What time does she get to school? 8:00
2. Will mows the grass at 6:00. It takes him 1 hour to finish. What time does he finish? 7:00
3. Susan bakes cookies at 2:00. It takes her a half-hour. What time do the cookies finish? 2:30
4. Tyler sweeps the floor at 12:00. It takes him a half-hour. What time does he finish? 12:30
5. Wendy watches a movie at 5:00. The movie lasts for 2 hours. What time does the movie finish? 7:00
6. Ken writes a story at 9:30. It takes him a half-hour. What time does he finish? 10:00

© Carson-Dellosa CD-2208 | Total Problems: | Total Correct: | Score: | 59

Name ______________________ **Calendars**

Fill in the calendar dates. Then, answer the questions on the lines provided. This month has 31 days. The first day of the month is Monday.

January

Sunday	Monday	Tuesday	Wednesday	Thursday	Friday	Saturday
	1	2	3	4	5	6
7	8	9	10	11	12	13
14	15	16	17	18	19	20
21	22	23	24	25	26	27
28	29	30	31			

1. How many Wednesdays are in January? 5
2. What day of the week is January 13? Saturday
3. How many Fridays are in January? 4
4. What day of the week is January 31? Wednesday
5. How many Tuesdays are in January? 5

60 | Total Problems: | Total Correct: | Score: | © Carson-Dellosa CD-2208

Name ______________________ **Calendars**

Fill in the calendar dates. Then, answer the questions on the lines provided. This month has 30 days. The first day of the month is Wednesday.

April

Sunday	Monday	Tuesday	Wednesday	Thursday	Friday	Saturday
			1	2	3	4
5	6	7	8	9	10	11
12	13	14	15	16	17	18
19	20	21	22	23	24	25
26	27	28	29	30		

1. How many Fridays are in April? 4
2. What day of the week is April 7? Tuesday
3. How many Mondays are in April? 4
4. Write the dates of the Mondays in April. 6, 13, 20, 27
5. What day of the week is April 10? Friday

 Total Problems: Total Correct: Score:

Name ______________________ **Calendars**

Fill in the calendar dates. Then, answer the questions on the lines provided. This month has 31 days. The first day of the month is Monday.

December

Sunday	Monday	Tuesday	Wednesday	Thursday	Friday	Saturday
	1	2	3	4	5	6
7	8	9	10	11	12	13
14	15	16	17	18	19	20
21	22	23	24	25	26	27
28	29	30	31			

1. What day of the week is December 4? Thursday
2. How many Wednesdays are in December? 5
3. What day of the week is December 20? Saturday
4. How many Fridays are in December? 4
5. What day of the week is December 31? Wednesday

 Total Problems: Total Correct: Score:

Name ______________________ **Nickels and Pennies**

Study the rule below. Then, count each group of coins. Write the amount on the line beside it.

Rule:

A penny equals 1 cent. 1¢

A nickel equals 5 cents. 5¢

1. 12 ¢
2. 9 ¢
3. 10 ¢
4. 11 ¢
5. 5 ¢

 Total Problems: Total Correct: Score:

Name ______________________ **Nickels and Pennies**

Count each group of coins. Write the amount on the line beside it.

1. 8 ¢
2. 17 ¢
3. 3 ¢
4. 6 ¢
5. 20 ¢
6. 21 ¢
7. 15 ¢
8. 4 ¢

 Total Problems: Total Correct: Score:

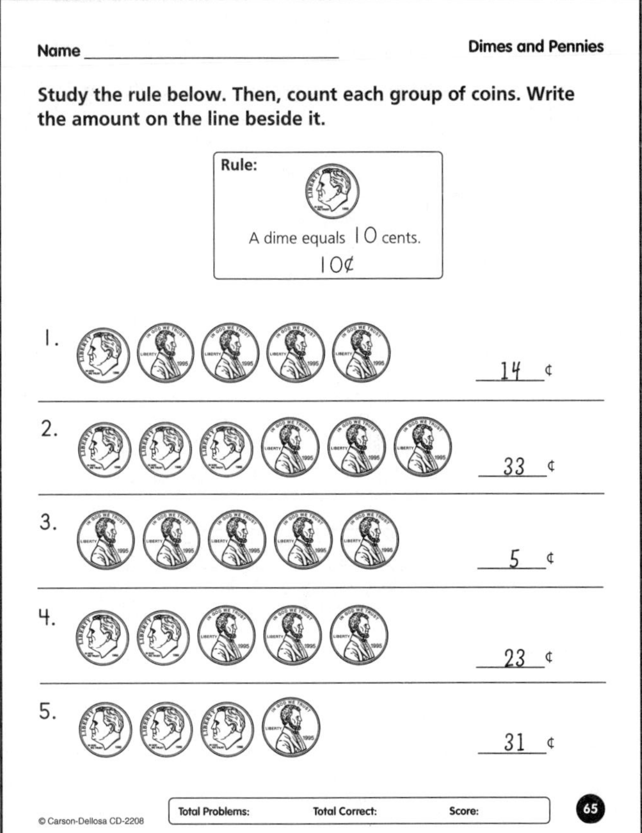

Name ______________________ **Dimes and Pennies**

Study the rule below. Then, count each group of coins. Write the amount on the line beside it.

Rule: A dime equals 10 cents. 10¢

1. 14 ¢
2. 33 ¢
3. 5 ¢
4. 23 ¢
5. 31 ¢

© Carson-Dellosa CD-2208 Total Problems: Total Correct: Score: 65

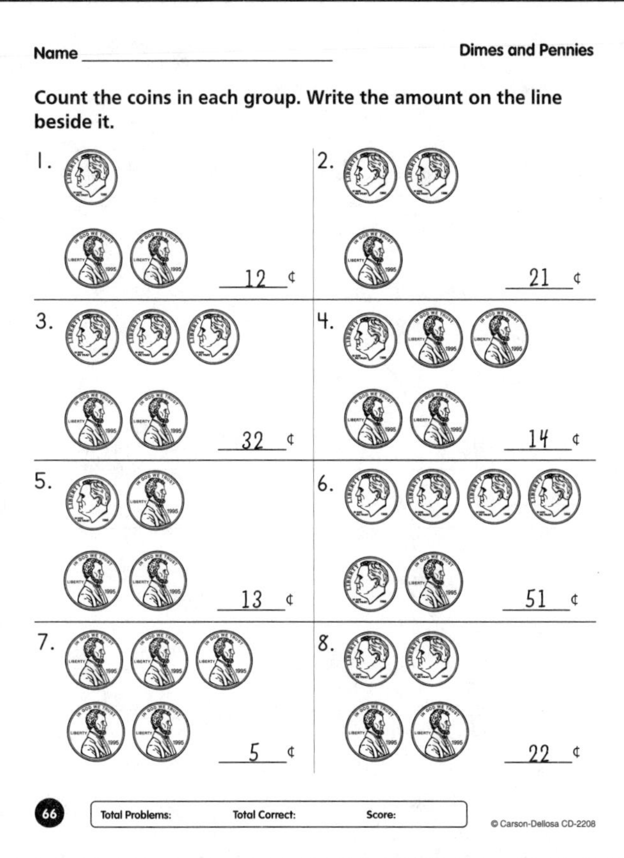

Name ______________________ **Dimes and Pennies**

Count the coins in each group. Write the amount on the line beside it.

1. 12 ¢
2. 21 ¢
3. 32 ¢
4. 14 ¢
5. 13 ¢
6. 51 ¢
7. 5 ¢
8. 22 ¢

66 Total Problems: Total Correct: Score: © Carson-Dellosa CD-2208

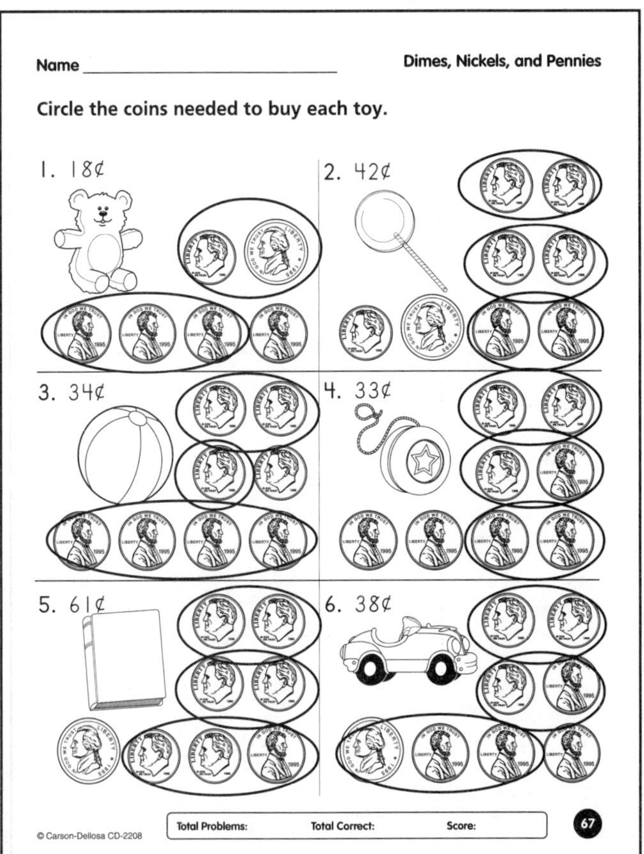

Name ______________________ **Dimes, Nickels, and Pennies**

Circle the coins needed to buy each toy.

1. 18¢
2. 42¢
3. 34¢
4. 33¢
5. 61¢
6. 38¢

© Carson-Dellosa CD-2208 Total Problems: Total Correct: Score: 67

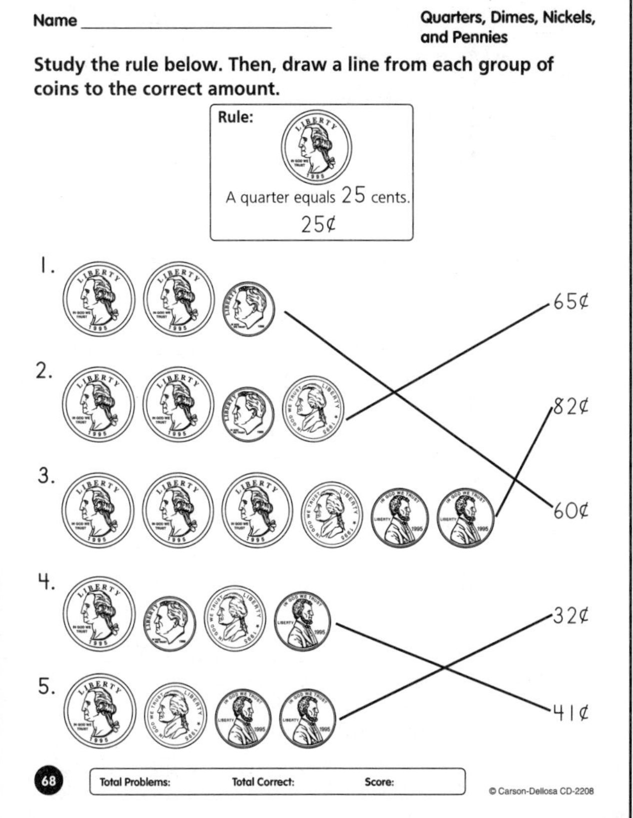

Name ______________________ **Quarters, Dimes, Nickels, and Pennies**

Study the rule below. Then, draw a line from each group of coins to the correct amount.

Rule: A quarter equals 25 cents. 25¢

1. 65¢
2. 82¢
3. 60¢
4. 32¢
5. 41¢

68 Total Problems: Total Correct: Score: © Carson-Dellosa CD-2208

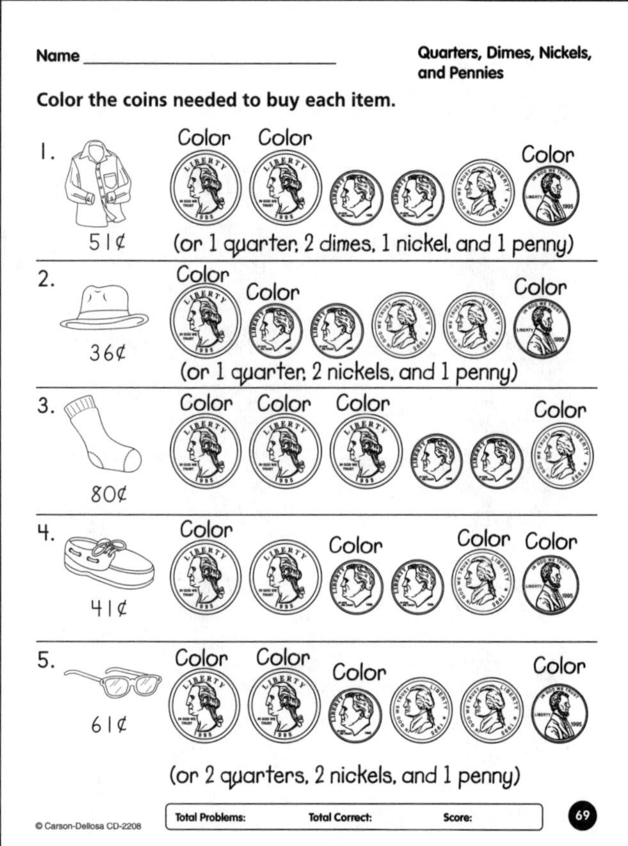

Name ______________________ Quarters, Dimes, Nickels, and Pennies

Color the coins needed to buy each item.

1. 51¢ — Color, Color, Color (or 1 quarter, 2 dimes, 1 nickel, and 1 penny)
2. 36¢ — Color, Color, Color (or 1 quarter, 2 nickels, and 1 penny)
3. 80¢ — Color, Color, Color, Color
4. 41¢ — Color, Color, Color, Color
5. 61¢ — Color, Color, Color, Color (or 2 quarters, 2 nickels, and 1 penny)

© Carson-Dellosa CD-2208 | Total Problems: | Total Correct: | Score: | 69

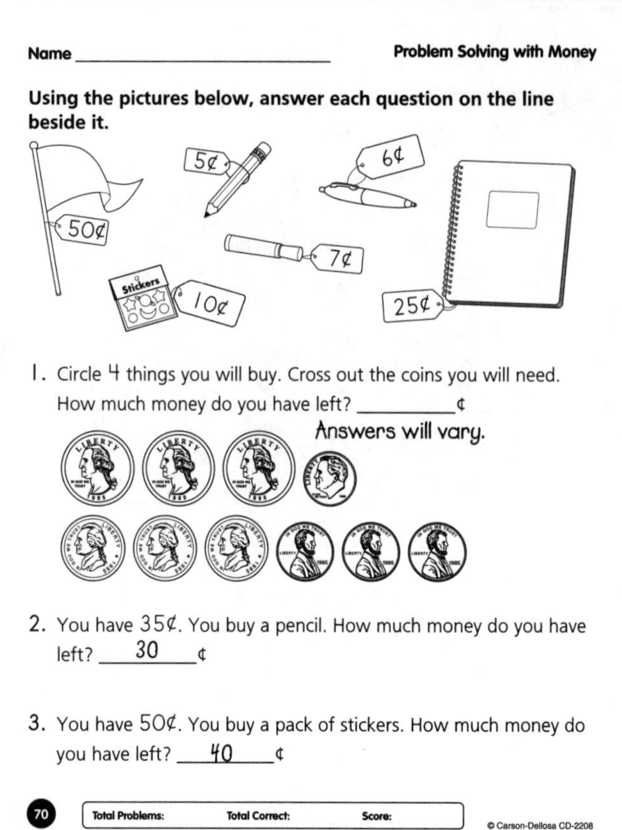

Name ______________________ Problem Solving with Money

Using the pictures below, answer each question on the line beside it.

1. Circle 4 things you will buy. Cross out the coins you will need. How much money do you have left? ________¢ Answers will vary.
2. You have 35¢. You buy a pencil. How much money do you have left? 30 ¢
3. You have 50¢. You buy a pack of stickers. How much money do you have left? 40 ¢

70 | Total Problems: | Total Correct: | Score: | © Carson-Dellosa CD-2208

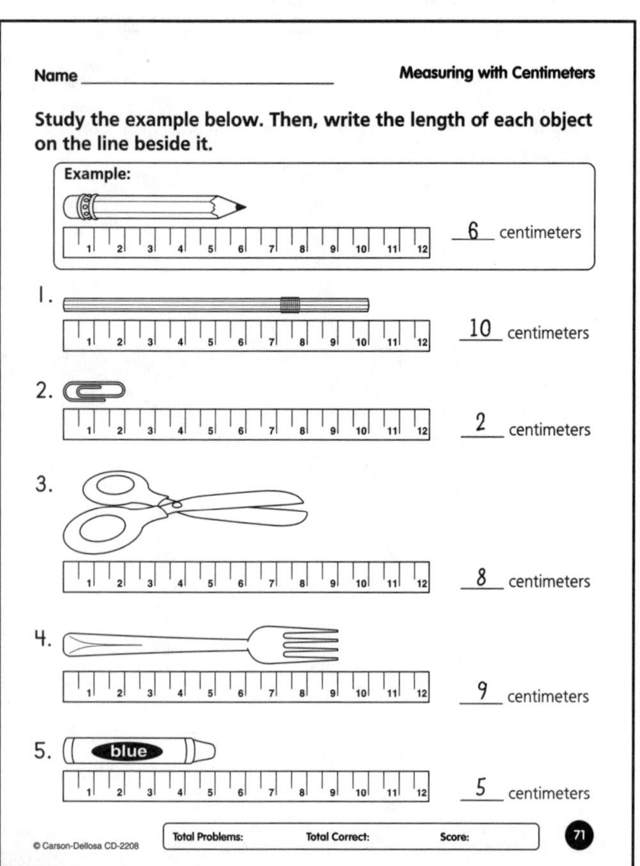

Name ______________________ Measuring with Centimeters

Study the example below. Then, write the length of each object on the line beside it.

Example: 6 centimeters

1. 10 centimeters
2. 2 centimeters
3. 8 centimeters
4. 9 centimeters
5. blue — 5 centimeters

© Carson-Dellosa CD-2208 | Total Problems: | Total Correct: | Score: | 71

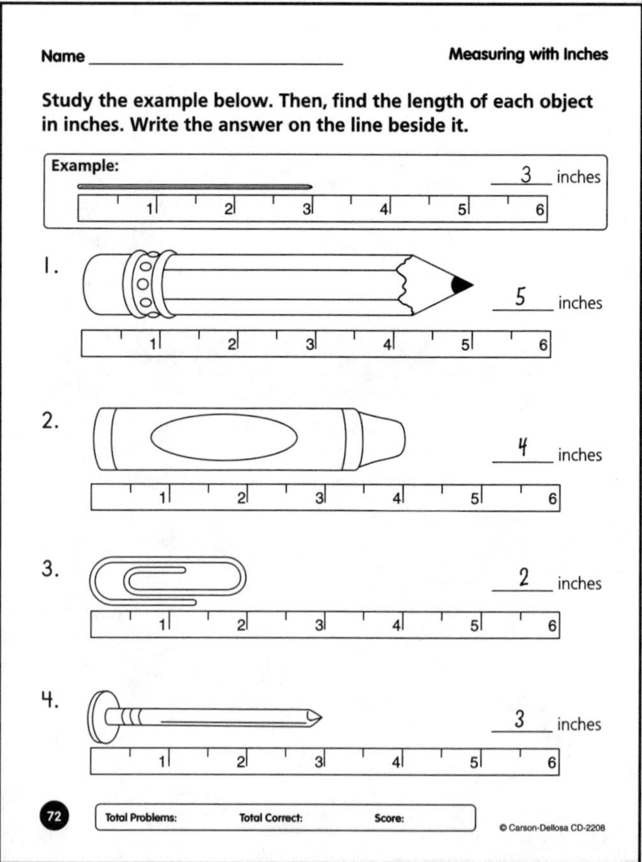

Name ______________________ Measuring with Inches

Study the example below. Then, find the length of each object in inches. Write the answer on the line beside it.

Example: 3 inches

1. 5 inches
2. 4 inches
3. 2 inches
4. 3 inches

72 | Total Problems: | Total Correct: | Score: | © Carson-Dellosa CD-2208

Name ____________________ **Identifying Plane Figures**

Study the examples below. Then, follow the directions for each problem.

Examples: Triangle, Circle, Rectangle

1. Color the triangles red. Color the circles blue. Color the rectangles green.

green, blue, red, green, blue, red, green, red

2. Count the shapes above. Write how many of each shape there are on the lines provided.

3 triangles 2 circles 3 rectangles

3. Color the circles yellow. Color the triangles orange. Color the rectangles red.

yellow, yellow, red, orange, yellow, red, yellow, orange, red, orange

4. Count the shapes above. Write how many of each shape there are on the lines provided.

3 triangles 4 circles 3 rectangles

© Carson-Dellosa CD-2208 | Total Problems: | Total Correct: | Score: | 73

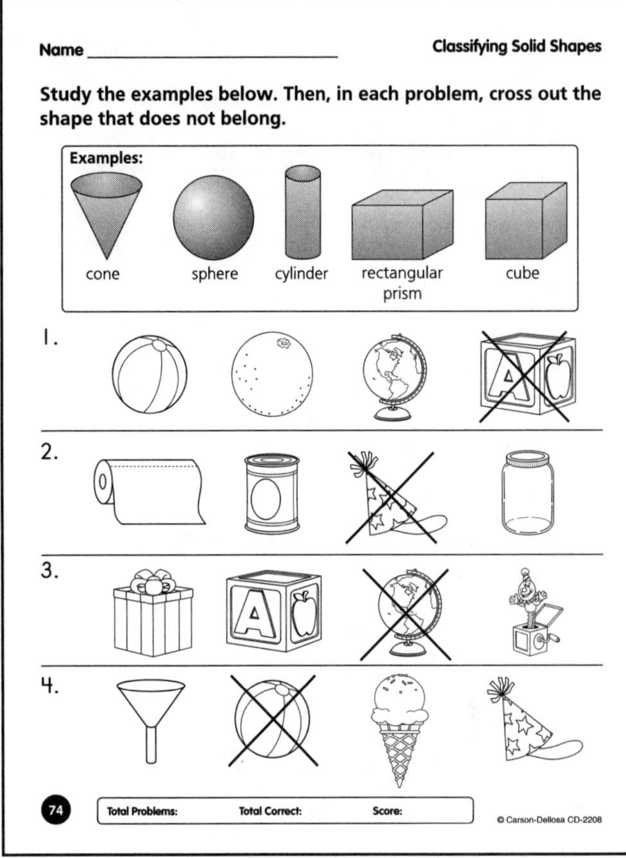

Name ____________________ **Pictographs**

Study the pictograph below and answer the questions on the lines provided.

Baseballs Owned by Five Friends

Friends	Number of Baseballs
Scott	⚾⚾⚾
Lindsey	⚾⚾⚾⚾⚾
Joe	⚾⚾⚾⚾
Sarah	⚾⚾⚾
Tim	⚾

1. How many baseballs does Tim have? 1
2. How many baseballs does Joe have? 4
3. How many baseballs do Scott and Sarah have in all? 3 + 3 = 6
4. How many baseballs do Tim, Joe, and Lindsey have in all? 1 + 4 + 5 = 10
5. How many more baseballs does Lindsey have than Joe? 5 – 4 = 1

© Carson-Dellosa CD-2208 | Total Problems: | Total Correct: | Score: | 75

Name ____________________ **Pictographs**

Study the pictograph below and answer the questions on the lines provided.

Cookies Sold by Ms. Ryall's First-Grade Class

Students	Boxes of Cookies
Mary	🍪🍪🍪🍪🍪🍪🍪
Cory	🍪🍪🍪
Lisa	🍪🍪🍪🍪🍪
Jill	🍪🍪🍪🍪
Lily	🍪🍪🍪🍪🍪🍪

Key: 🍪 = 1 box of cookies

1. How many boxes of cookies did Jill sell? 4
2. How many boxes of cookies did Mary sell? 7
3. Who sold the most boxes of cookies? Mary
4. Who sold the fewest boxes of cookies? Cory
5. How many more boxes did Lily sell than Cory? 6 – 3 = 3

76 | Total Problems: | Total Correct: | Score: | © Carson-Dellosa CD-2208

Name ____________ **Bar Graphs**

Study the bar graph and answer the questions on the lines provided.

Sports Liked by First Graders

Sports	Number of First Graders
baseball	4
basketball	3
tennis	2
golf	1
football	4
soccer	5

1. How many first graders like golf? 1
2. How many first graders like baseball? 4
3. How many first graders like baseball and tennis?
   4 + 2 = 6
4. Which sport do first graders like the least?
   golf
5. How many more first graders like soccer than tennis?
   5 - 2 = 3

Total Problems: Total Correct: Score:

Name ____________ **Pie Charts**

Study the pie chart and answer the questions on the lines provided.

Animals in the Zoo

15 bears
15 lions
10 giraffes
20 snakes

1. How many bears are in the zoo? 15
2. How many lions are in the zoo? 15
3. How many snakes are in the zoo? 20
4. The zoo has 15 of which animal(s)? bears, lions
5. The zoo has the most of which animal? snakes

Total Problems: Total Correct: Score: